WOMAN TO WOMAN

Also by Elizabeth Bookser Barkley

Loving the Everyday: Meditations for Moms

Elizabeth Bookser Barkley

Woman to Woman

SEEING GOD IN DAILY LIFE

ST. ANTHONY MESSENGER PRESS

Cincinnati, Ohio

Scripture citations are taken from *The New Revised Standard Version of the Bible*, copyright ©1989 by the Division of Christian Education of the National Council of the Churches of Christ in the United States, and are used by permission. All rights reserved.

Reprinted by permission of the publishers and the Trustees of Amherst College from *The Poems of Emily Dickinson*, Thomas H. Johnson, ed., Cambridge, Massachusetts: The Belknap Press of Harvard University Press, copyright ©1951, 1955, 1979, 1983 by the President and Fellows of Harvard College.

The excerpt from "Life-Hook" by Juana de Ibarbourou, in *Open to the Sun: A Bilingual Anthology of Latin-American Women Poets*, edited and translated by Nora Jacquez Wieser (Perivale Press, 1979), is reprinted by permission of Lawrence P. Springarn.

Cover illustration by Steve Erspamer, S.M.
Cover design by Mary Alfieri
Book design by Julie Lonneman
Electronic format and pagination by Sandra Digman

ISBN 0-86716-226-0

Published by St. Anthony Messenger Press
Printed in the U.S.A.

ॐ TO ALL THE SPECIAL WOMEN in my life
who have walked with me on my journey
toward holiness, especially my mother,
my sisters, my daughters and
my friends

Contents

Renewing Our Spirits

Introduction

Dizzying and blurred, intricate and tangled, life catches us up in its complexities. Around us, events converge to threaten our peace. Illness, fragmented relationships, accidental injuries, deliberate hurts hover nearby. Life, once neat and harmonious, sometimes seems out of control.

Counselors, self-help books, aerobic exercise regimens help chase away the blues. They lift us temporarily; still, many women feel a void in their lives.

Being a woman was simpler in centuries past. Roles clearly defined gave a structure to daily living: rising before dawn, working the fields, caring for children, preparing meals, keeping the hearth warm and the home safe. Even prayer fit neatly into the limitations of each day. In the field, women paused for prayer at the tolling of the church bells in the middle of a busy day, unembarrassed at sincere and public piety. In a culture where God was a given, women had daily reminders that they were dependent not only on others, but on a Being beyond time and gender.

Though they're not so apparent, reminders of the transcendent abound in the lives of women today. These

God-glimmers prompt us to get in touch with the divine within and without. But we have to know where to find them. In a culture that sometimes scoffs at the notion of the spiritual, God appears not in wind and burning bushes but in gentle nudges. If we're tuned in, and some of the noise is tuned out, we can tap into our springs of spirituality.

There are others seeking the same inner tranquility, who want to be grounded in something deeper. For centuries, even well into the twentieth, women gravitated toward other women in their quest for spiritual fulfillment. Religious congregations flourished as young women attached themselves to those who modeled spirituality and sanctity. Today the numbers of vowed religious are fewer, but woman's search goes on in other ways: in prayer groups for mothers of young children; in small faith communities where women—young and old, married and single—reach out candidly for support; through cyberspace talk groups as women separated by continents share their spiritual hunger.

This book makes no claims about being the last word in defining women's spirituality. It is a beginning, a simple goodwill offering from one woman to others. I have not limited my reflections to what some might consider "spiritual" topics, since my personal spirituality veers toward the incarnational, acknowledging the sacredness in all that is human. These reflections flow from my daily experiences of being a woman and trying to integrate those experiences into my search for holiness. Many of the issues and incidents I explore could apply to both men and women; it's the perspective, not the topics, that orients these meditations toward women.

These pages don't define failproof theological principles, but offer stories and insights from my life as a woman to other women seeking nourishment for their spirits. I hope for those hungering for whole and holy lives it offers a little glimmer of God to lighten, and enlighten, the journey.

I'm grateful to the staff of St. Anthony Messenger Press for inviting me to write another book on a topic close to my heart, and for being flexible as I wrestled with its form. Thanks also to my friends who provided feedback on drafts of the book: Bonnie Finn, Susan Hines-Brigger and Mary Ann Schlomer.

Friendships

O how glad I should be to have your arm around me &
my arm around you & to walk with you again...—1849
letter from Antoinette Brown to Lucy Stone

W alking together arm in arm—what a perfect snapshot of true friendship. A century earlier, when Antoinette Brown and Lucy Stone lived, women's friendships were more physical and more demonstrative than today's hands-off culture allows. But I'm certain they were no deeper. Rather than embracing physically, my friends link themselves to my heart and my soul in our mutual walk toward God. They help me see more clearly, to refocus the sometimes-blurred essentials of life.

Forget the small talk when a friend calls mid-morning on a day set aside to work through piles of unanswered memos and unfinished tasks. Her "How are you doing?" calls out of me a stream of concerns articulated to no one else, barely explored within my own heart. "Where'd that all come from?" I wonder later, feeling relief at having sorted through the mish-mash of feelings I hardly knew I harbored. Within a few minutes, with barely a prod, she had unplugged some inner confusion and had listened as I worked through it aloud. She had called to set a date for dinner, which we finally remembered to do, but more importantly, her call had been therapeutic and affirming.

Recently a colleague, overwhelmed with projects at work and the demands of raising a family, told me of her rediscovery of female friends after years of neglect. Although she had thought she couldn't afford to take time to be with friends, what she realized was how much energy she took back to her family and work after evenings of friendship.

Some women never move out of the friendship habit, like those I've met from several neighborhoods in my city. As I got to know more about them through college and career days, I was intrigued by the recurring mention of "club." Not "our club" or "my bridge club," merely "club." What was "club," I wondered. Having to ask exposed me as an outsider. "Club is just club," one tried to explain as she told me it was her turn to host "club" at her home. What did women do? Nothing structured like playing board games or discussing books; it was the being, not the doing, that was important. Happily for them, it was an easy transition out of teenage and college years into club, a phenomenon that, as far as I could determine, ended only when the members were too frail to continue the tradition.

Sometimes I envied this tradition that was such a natural part of their growing up and so comfortable to be a part of. Having moved away from my hometown after high school and having not grown up in the tradition of "club," I realized almost too late that time was eroding some friendships that had been important to me. During the early years of raising a family, these friendships survived mostly through hurried phone calls, hastily written cards or an occasional meal out.

Realizing, like my friend from work, that my life would be richer for my women friends, I vowed to make space to renew the bonds that renew me. Early morning is my favorite friendship space. Rising sometimes before the sun does, I throw on any old clothes—true friends don't mind— and we rendezvous over hot muffins or eggs or goetta, a dish I now recall we both learned to savor through a mutual friend. Only the hearty join us at that hour. Pots of coffee later, we've caught up on career changes and frustrations, health of families and friends, world issues, and life's small tragedies and amusing twists.

Earlier in the meal, the rising sun had bothered me enough to force me to shift positions. Now, turning to check on the sun, I'm caught off guard by the crowds at tables and in the lobby. When had they arrived?

My friend's "arm around me" and mine around her, we had shut out a world of distractions for an embrace of friendship, one that warmed me even more than the sun whose progress up the sky reminded me this meal must end...until the next time we would claim a space for an early morning friendship "walk."

&♣ BEGINNING TODAY... I will take time out of my busyness to slow down for the business of friendship. If I belong to a club or a longtime group of friends, I will clear my calendar for the next gathering. Or I will call a friend I've been neglecting and catch up on her life or make a date to share a meal and a slice of my life with her.

Being Dependent

Take good care of yourself over these next few weeks. Let your family give to you—this isn't an easy thing to do, as I'm sure you know.—Note on a card from a friend

Many women need to be more dependent. Including me. I can't believe I'm writing these words. An avowed feminist, constantly promoting self-reliance and independence, I've seen too many women defeated by dependence—on boyfriends, parents, husbands, authority figures in schools and business. Still, many of us need to be needed less, we need to need more.

Women are the givers of the world. Whether it's innate or cultural, we gravitate toward nurturing and managing the details of life. Some of us are more natural or skilled in this role, the women that others turn to when they need someone to kiss a hurt and make it better or comfort those who need spiritual relief. And it's usually women who make certain the kitchen cupboards and refrigerator are full, the office coffeepot has been scrubbed before a new pot is brewed, the rooms have been reserved a year ahead for monthly meetings.

So, as my friend warned me in her get-well card sent before my surgery, I would have to do an about-face as I recuperated, letting family and friends give to me, a role I surely was unused to.

But I had no choice. It was not major surgery, or life-threatening, so I was sure it was merely a matter of willpower and I would be my old self in no time. But my body fooled me. I was reduced to weeks of dependence. Someone else would have to address the Christmas cards, buy the stamps and mail the packages. Friends and relatives brought homemade meals, called to monitor my progress, cautioned me about getting too rambunctious as I began to regain my strength.

And they sent cards. Funny cards, empathetic cards, cards with personal and loving notes, cards that showed me that being dependent wasn't the negative experience I had anticipated. It was the cards that opened my eyes. The cards made me see how important it was to step out of my independent mode every once in a while, to experience being recipient rather than sender. Only with this experience could I be more compassionate, more whole as a woman. My nurturing side had been working overtime for years; I needed some balance in my life.

And some empathy. I needed to feel how many women around me feel daily—sick in body (but more importantly in spirit), powerless, needy...in a word, dependent. It was no accident that my experience of dependence came at one of the busiest times of year, right before Christmas. No accident in that I had agreed on a surgery date in mid-December because it best fit into my teaching schedule when classes were suspended for a few weeks; in this detail of scheduling I had asserted control, my independence. It was no accident in a more providential sense that this experience of dependence tied in so perfectly with the Scripture readings of the season.

Another woman, who figures so prominently in the Christmas story, has modeled dependence for centuries. "Here am I, the servant of the Lord; let it be with me according to your word," the mystified Mary had said to the angel announcing that she was to bear the savior. In Mary's song of praise, after visiting her cousin Elizabeth, we hear another challenge to independence: "He has brought down the powerful from their thrones, and lifted up the lowly." And when it was time to give birth (we can only imagine the dependence she experienced, since the male evangelists skip details a woman writer surely would have included), she "laid him in a manger, because there was no place for them in the inn."

For some women, these passages could be unsettling, corroborating the centuries-old position that women should be passive vessels. But that interpretation fails to look at the other glimpses we have of Mary: being independent enough to allow her young son to move into an itinerant ministry to which he was called when she could have clung to him in dependence as he grew into manhood, being strong enough to stand by him (in sadness and empathy) at the cross, to go on with her life and the life of the new Church after his death.

Dependence and independence should be shadow sides of a full life. For many women, because they've never tasted the joys of being independent, that balance is still to come. But for those of us too used to being on top of the world, on the giving end, an occasional experience of neediness is called for. The word "pathos," the root of empathy, crops up in a number of other words. One word it calls to mind is pathetic, but I prefer to move in the direction of passion. Once I've been dependent, I can move back into my independence with a passion, to feel with those less powerful, to recall my experience (so positive only because it was temporary) as I encourage them out of their dependence.

&❧ BEGINNING TODAY... I will allow myself experiences of

dependence by letting others in on the joys of nurturing me. I will also take little steps to help women who seem trapped in relationships of permanent dependence, so they can experience the fullness of womanhood, as not only dependent but also independent.

Mothers and Daughters

Mom, thanks for all you've done for me. You don't know how big an impact you've had on my life.—Inscription in a book from my daughter

My aging mother lay in her hospital bed, recovering from surgery, surrounded by the paraphernalia of medicine—a heart monitor, tubes to the oxygen supply, sterile tape and bandages, a thermometer, a water jug and a drab box of institutional tissues. Hooked up to a breathing machine for one of her periodic treatments to strengthen her lungs, she could not speak to me sitting on the bottom of her bed. The lack of communication with her, the impersonality of the room frustrated me. Then my eye caught the bottle of lotion.

The lotion, the perfect solution. I opened it, squeezed a few thick drops on my hands and began massaging it into her feet. Now we were connected, not only physically, but emotionally, as the experience transported me vividly back to mother-daughter bonds of my childhood. Smells, noises, textures came rushing back as I remembered my mother's favorite way to relax: a foot rub from her daughter. In my youth, I was mildly repulsed by the whole affair, but she took such pleasure in it after a long day on her feet, and I was lured by the prospect of profit (a nickel, a quarter—whatever the going rate for foot rubs was at the time), that I participated in the ritual.

Along with the physical contact came contact of another sort as we shared her favorite television shows, always musical programs featuring her favorite entertainers like Lawrence Welk or Perry Como. In truth, they became my favorites, too, though I'd never have admitted it then to my friends for fear they'd think me strange in my adult tastes.

Now decades later, the bond had been revived, but with a slight twist: Then I had been daughter, dependent for nurturing upon my mother; now, in her age and illness, I was nurturing her. But not exactly, or not completely. Over the years, the roles had subtly shifted, but the daughter role, though it may change, can never be completely discarded.

It's such a complicated relationship, one that can snare the daughter into a web of continual dependence or one that can weave two now-adult lives together in an inseparable bond of friendship. I've watched friends struggle with the role transitions that maturing demands. Once "under mother's thumb," as emerging adults they try out new modes of relating as they begin to realize that the obedient (or rebellious) daughter role no longer seems to fit. The answer to the mother's "How are you?" as they embrace in person or over the phone depends on how much the mother is willing to give up and how much the daughter is willing to risk in forging a mature relationship.

Some pairs move easily into a new bond, a friendship that has a head start on all the others a young woman may have formed, since these "new" friends have known each other even from before the daughter's birth. "My mom's my best friend," I've heard often. "There's nothing we don't share."

Other daughters never make that dramatic a leap, but begin to relax the formerly rigid lines of demarcation between motherhood and friendship as they share more adult joys and sorrows: the birth of children, buying a new home, losing a job, grieving over hurting or lost love relationships, burying the man who was father to one and husband to the other.

Yet some women never manage to figure out how to shed their child-daughter selves for ones more fitting their age, or they've never been granted permission by mothers who can't give up the control the former relationship allowed. These daughters wander their adult lives in a limbo that denies them the richness of sharing present joys and sorrows with a woman who is responsible for so much of their past, no matter how confused or traumatic it might have been.

Even if we've managed to adjust to being adults in the presence of our mothers, we will always be our mother's daughters. And no matter how full our mothers' lives have become once their maternal nests have emptied, they will always be our mothers.

My own mother, admirable in her willingness to step back and allow me to make choices, make mistakes, make a mark in life, still mothers me. It's a tribute to her sensitivity to my sensitivity that she mothers me in such a way that I welcome rather than avoid her ministerings.

No soup tastes quite as good as a bowl prepared in her kitchen, even if it's out of a can identical to one from my own cupboard. No nap is quite as peaceful and snugly as one on her couch. No advice is quite as relevant as what she shares out of her wisdom and experience, whether or not I choose to follow it.

Even in her nearly total dependence in illness, as I leave for the several-hours' drive home, she urges my father to send along some fruit from their cellar. I may be leaving her physically, but she's still concerned about my health.

"I'll pray you safely home," she says as she kisses me good-bye, acknowledging that even though I had grown up in the house where she and my father still live, I have made a new home for myself apart from theirs.

I nod my thanks, as she gets the last nurturing word. To the hospital staff hovering around her bed she may be just another patient, but though she looks tired and frail propped up on pillows in the bed, she manages the grace to act like a mother to me. I feel blessed and daughterly knowing she carries me in her heart.

❧ BEGINNING TODAY... I will think of some special way to thank my mother for her influence in my life, by calling to chat with her on the phone, sending her flowers or stopping in for a surprise visit. If my memories of our past relationship are negative, I will focus on the present as I reach out to her. If my mother is no longer alive, I will take time to look through pictures or memorabilia that remind me of her, and say a prayer of gratitude for the years we shared as mother and daughter.

Siblings

How very good and pleasant it is when kindred live together in unity!—Psalm 133:1

"I've just lost my best friend." The words, spoken by a grieving woman standing not far from the coffin of her sister, startled me in their familiarity, since I had witnessed a similar scene and heard similar words a few months earlier, in a funeral home several states away. What was this bond that grappled soul to soul in sibling fidelity, that linked two together in a way that spouses or only-children could never comprehend?

Because both women who had spoken the words had lived near their sisters, physical closeness had not been a barrier to maintaining a deep friendship. Other siblings, not close enough for daily contact, nurture their sibling love-bonds resistant to the cleavage of distance, life-style or geography.

My aunt, for instance. Separated in age by almost a decade and in proximity by hundreds of miles, she radiates love for her "brudder dear," as she affectionately calls my father. Despite our efforts to weasel out of her some offense he committed in his over seven decades of life, she maintains he is and always has been the perfect boy/man/brother..."except," she says with a twinkle in her eyes as she turns them admiringly toward him, "except the time we had to send him to the pantry."

That bond, resilient in the face of the death of their father, mother and brothers, takes on a holiness in its devotion. Their love speaks of something beyond the mere natural. A few years earlier, she related to me recently, residents of a home where she was living noticed that reverence between brother and sister. "They thought we were Amish or some other religious group," my aunt, a lifelong Lutheran, chuckled, "because I would call him 'brother' and he would call me 'sister.'"

To hear her tell it, that sense of awe had always marked their relationship. Not so with my own sibling history. On first reflection, my childhood as one of six children was fraught more often with warfare than wonder. But remembering more carefully, I cull forth images of deep loyalty and attachment, hallmarks of our adult sibling years. Like those clandestine trips during adolescence to the local fast-food restaurant for milk shakes and fries, though my oldest sister had been told to come straight home ("Squeal and I'll never drive you anywhere again"). Or the homework support another sister and I, who shared many high school classes, offered one another. I, the writer, she the scientist and mathematician—we had too much integrity to actually divulge the answers, but as I labored over an unsolvable science problem, a wave of enlightenment and relief would sweep over me when she'd drop her casual hint, "Why don't you try this formula?"

Today in our maturity and in the diversity of our lives and interests, the six of us remain loyal and caring and fiercely protective of each other. Is one ill? Our cards and calls and surprise flowers can help restore health. Is one burdened financially? Subtly, aware of the need to maintain dignity, we share from our own surplus...and expect the same in return.

Families differ in their needs to maintain these sibling relationships. For some, being scattered among cities would be devastating, accustomed as they are to each other's friendship and feedback. Daily phone calls or impromptu visits for a cup of tea and a dose of advice shape their days that would be empty without this intimate contact. In other families, where too much togetherness strains fragile bonds, occasional gatherings are enough to refuel family love.

In my youth, striving to assert my individuality among a sea of sisters, I was eager to distance myself from them. At that time, I was blind to the bonds, physical and spiritual, that I realize, only in retrospect, enriched my life. I now know that for me distancing was important. Just as children need the time and experience to establish independence from parents, the same can be true about sometimes restricting and long-established patterns among siblings. Will the firstborn allow others to take charge and make decisions? Will those five or ten years older ever permit the youngest to grow out of the role as "baby" and become their peer? In times of crisis, especially when the health of their parents is threatened, will those family ties be further strengthened or will they snap?

Maintaining sibling relations takes time and commitment. We can nurture them or allow them to stagnate, just like friendships or marriages. But whether we welcome or resist them, there's no extricating ourselves from the common threads that weave our siblings into the intricate and often complicated web of our adult family lives.

&❧ BEGINNING TODAY... I will call from my memory images of myself and my siblings. Perhaps my memories of growing up with them are not all pleasant and I harbor some resentment. Perhaps as adults we have been in conflict—over money, parents, child-rearing. If so, I will try to come to peace with whatever negative feelings I still carry within me. Whether our relation has been harmonious or hassled, I will tuck my siblings into my prayers today, grateful for their influence on my life.

Love That Endures

Love's not time's fool, though rosy lips and cheeks
Within his bending sickle's compass come;
Love alters not with his brief hours and weeks,
But bears it out even to the edge of doom.
—*William Shakespeare*, "Sonnet 116"

T he day was ordinary enough, a warm March day that held promise of thawing the snow-covered ground. The occasion was anything but ordinary.

I had arrived at my parents' home on a far-too-infrequent visit. The next day was their wedding anniversary—fifty-two years. Although that day would hold the real celebration—Mass at their parish, breakfast with a friend, an afternoon concert and dinner—they had already begun to celebrate.

I had accompanied my father to the florist for flowers, a corsage and a bouquet of eight flowers—six yellow roses for their children, the evidence of their love, and two irises, purple tinged with yellow.

As my mother prepared lunch, strains of World War II-era songs drifted into the kitchen. These were the songs of their courtship and brief honeymoon that official orders to "ship out" had abruptly interrupted, songs the pilots had listened to in faraway Burma as they longed for an end to the war. It was the music that reminded my parents of their youthful love, the perfect music for an impromptu anniversary dance.

Not as sure on their feet as they had been fifty-two years earlier, they danced in socks and slippers as I watched, a privileged spectator to the sacredness of their love, my father caressing my mother's newly-coifed hair with gentle kisses.

I remember witnessing their love in my childhood, embarrassed by their dinnertime hugs and kisses in our kitchen, a chorus member as they sang their favorite songs—"Always" or "Let Me Call You Sweetheart." Still, even as an adult, I can never know the depth and details of their love. What was it like to be young and pregnant, give birth to a first child while your husband was at war? How did they maintain their love, and their dignity, during lean years with six children to clothe, feed and educate? Will we children ever decipher the meaning of the mysterious four-letter code written near their names on every birthday, anniversary, Valentine and Christmas card since their love began?

Each love relationship has its own mysteries and rhythms, in its beginnings the same, but somehow different, from love that has been tempered and tried by time. In the early stages of my love for my husband-to-be, I built my days around anticipated phone calls, cards, nights out together. Each would cause a surge of excitement, a rush of love that consumed my thoughts and feelings. This will pass, I realized, as we spend more time together and grow accustomed to one another. Knowing I might be naive, I hoped we would never take each other and our love for granted.

And we haven't. Our own marriage of twenty-plus years, though not as seasoned as my parents', is a cause for celebration and possibly a source of mystery to our children. We have our own rituals, like the Christmas ornament with a trio of creatures for our three children, and our inside jokes. A glance across the table or a poke in the side sends a message that we remember the original joke or occasion that triggered our mutual memory. When we laugh, our children accuse us of laughing at them; we can never explain to their satisfaction that these memories have taken on a life of their own shared only by the two of us.

Births, deaths, challenges of new jobs and tensions in old ones, marriages and divorces among friends, each child's first steps and first words—threads of a bond so interwoven that they seem to disappear in the tapestry of our lives together.

Alone, we would never have survived the crises or savored the seemingly insignificant joys. On our wedding day we vowed to support one another in our journey toward God. When we announced our vows in the thrill of new love, we could only sense their meaning. We've come to grasp the implications of those vows as we've lived them year by year. Today, we're still unsure of what the future will bring. But like our parents who modeled fidelity for us, we pray that our commitment to one another, blessed many years ago, will continue to be a source of strength for us and an inspiration, and mystery, to our children.

ᔥ BEGINNING TODAY... I will reflect on the value of committed married love in my own life or in the lives of my parents, my married friends, or my married children. I will pray for continued growth, perseverance and love in these marriages.

The Cycle of Life

And the Word became flesh and lived among us.
—*John 1:14*

N avajo mythology includes a figure named, appropriately, Changing Woman, the embodiment of the cyclical nature of life. Unfamiliar with any image so descriptive in my own heritage, I've gravitated toward her as I reflect on the rhythms of my woman's body.

As a teen, with the onset of menstruation, I came to dread what my girlfriends and I referred to as the monthly "curse." With increasing regularity, I charted the days of cramps and curtailed activity. After waiting so long to become a woman, I began to wonder whether womanhood hadn't been a bit overrated by my foremothers.

As I matured and grew used to my predictable woman's body, tracking my menstrual cycles gave me a sense of security. I learned to read the first signs of the arrival of my monthly "visitor," by now more welcomed than feared. Although at times annoying, the slight pain each month was, in a strange sense, a companion affirming my health and my solidarity with other women.

While it's not often a subject of conversation, menstruation provides an unspoken link with every other woman of every generation. Not every woman will be a mother, but every woman experiences this rhythmic bond with the earth—each woman a "changing woman."

For some women, the burden of menstruation may be its irregularity and unpredictability, but there's still a rhythm to connect to. Though menstrual periods may not always be as regular as the cycle of the moon, or the ebb and flow of currents, there's still a predictability about this physical change, like the gradual change of seasons, which can never be tied to particular dates on the calendar, but are always certain to arrive.

And for those who do bear children, it's the deviation from this predictable rhythm that first signals new life within. "My period's late"—three words that usually introduce a whole new body experience to a woman. Already in tune with subtle monthly changes before she became pregnant, now the soon-to-be-mother becomes more deeply a "changing woman." From recognizing which foods don't sit well in a stomach squished by her baby's growing body to noting the frequency and intensity of the first contractions of labor, she learns to read the body that now harbors a life that could not survive outside her own. The task she's about to undertake, easing the baby from the warmth and security of her womb to the reality of a separate existence, has been foreshadowed by years of recurring monthly pain.

Not that she can ever be fully prepared. Despite promises of the soothing effect of regular "cleansing breaths" and back rubs by devoted labor "coaches," I've met no woman who fully anticipated the pain of birth. In labor with my second child, as I watched the bedside monitor register the intensity of my contractions, I was overcome with a sense of dejà vu: "Ah, now I remember!" How could I have forgotten, in less than three years, at that?

A few hours later, the answer became perfectly clear as I watched the nurses hand my husband our second child, and then snuggled her next to me before they whisked her away for afterbirth care. A new life, and a daughter at that! Before I knew it, she'd be keeping her own calendar of menstrual cycles, and she'd be complaining, like teenagers for generations, about the inconvenience of being a woman.

If she would listen, if she wouldn't consider it too corny or too poetic, I would share with her my love affair with being a woman. "The Word became flesh" not that we should despise the flesh but that we should embrace it. I would tell her that the pains of a woman's body are nothing compared with its unfathomable miracles and incredible surprises.

But now's not the time. Maybe never. But even if I never tell her, she'll learn, just as I've learned, about the ever-changing yet curiously changeless burden-gift, one that links her to women across cultures and generations.

❧ BEGINNING TODAY... I will embrace the rhythms of menstruation as a bond to other women. Whether my periods are regular or irregular, painful or painless, I will take time to realize that this part of my life as a "changing woman" is one of the few universals separating me from men and connecting me to my sisters throughout the world.

Body Images

Do you not know that you are God's temple and that
God's Spirit dwells in you?—1 Corinthians 3:16

As she lay in the hospital emergency room, her arm severed below the elbow, my young friend groaned in pain. But the pain went beyond the physical. Her whole self-image had been shattered with the loss of a limb. A freak accident had, from her vantage point, transformed her into a freak.

Like many young women, she had so intricately fused her image of body with her image of self that an apparent flaw in one jeopardized the integrity of the other. She had been active, she had been attractive, she had been sexy. Would she ever be again? And was it fair to expect her husband of a few months, who had married a "whole" woman, to be faithful to this new person, now a limb less than the one he had married?

Over the course of a few months, I watched another talented young woman nearly starve herself to death through anorexia. Not privy to the details, but assured that she was getting counseling, I recoiled at the transmutation from a self-assured woman to one barely recognizable, her shrinking body hidden under layers of bulky clothing, a sort of camouflage masking the pain she was enduring.

Today these women are healthy and whole. Sometimes the one sports a prosthetic arm, but feels comfortable without it. Prayer, therapy and her husband's devotion helped her find her inner wholeness. Her accident led to a career change prompted by self-reflection about who she really was and what she wanted to be. Not long ago, I watched with satisfaction as a local television station profiled her work as a high school religion teacher. Her students had written and collected so many letters of praise about their teacher that the news producers realized this woman, whole in the truest sense of the word, was someone worth sharing with their viewers.

Recently I encountered the other young woman in the lobby of the college where I had taught her. Although I had known she was on her way to recovery, I could now feel confident that her body crisis was well in the past. Bubbling with enthusiasm about her elementary school class, she looked healthy...and slightly pudgy by the standards she no longer holds herself to. She was beaming with fulfillment as a teacher and a wife.

For both young women, initially painful stories are being rewritten with more satisfying endings than they might have predicted a few years ago. Both have confronted the demons of "the ideal body" and emerged victorious.

Not so with many others. Bombarded with provocative billboard ads for jeans and perfume, distracted by voluptuous models falling out of skimpy swimsuits on magazines stacked enticingly at checkout lanes, teased cruelly by friends (who should know how their words sting) about muscular thighs or flabby upper arms, young women wallow in self-loathing. Never mind that they've made the dean's list or logged the most volunteer hours at a community hospital or can outrun the neighborhood boys on the soccer field. Their body is their all.

And it's not just a plague of the young. A trim middle-aged woman, commenting on how overweight some of her high school classmates appeared at a class reunion, remarked that they were her inspiration. "I look at them and I spend one more hour on the treadmill."

An apt image for the body battle many women face. Obsessed with meeting some cultural ideal that no one has clearly defined or proved healthful, they expend energy but go nowhere in their quest for bodily perfection. They build their schedules around health clubs and their meals around liquid diets in a can. They measure their self-worth in things lost—inches and pounds—rather than things gained.

The human body, precious because God chose to redeem us as the Word incarnate, has rightly been called a temple. But temples should be precious not for themselves, but for the treasures they enshrine. Too many of us confuse the temple with the treasure. Occasionally we need to distance ourselves from our scales, our exercise bikes, our calorie counters. True, none of these is essentially harmful, but collectively they distract us from a more fulfilling and sacred mission in life: unearthing and sharing the true treasure within us.

❧ BEGINNING TODAY... I will look around at the women in my life who are special to me. I will note their bodily "imperfections," then reflect on how insignificant these external flaws are when measured against the inner beauty of these women. Next, I will reflect on how they see me in the same light, even though I may sometimes be fixated on my physical flaws.

To Your Health

Have you seen the fool that corrupted his own live body?
or the fool that corrupted her own live body?
For they do not conceal themselves, and cannot conceal
themselves.—Walt Whitman, "I Sing the Body Electric"

Too often it takes a crisis for women to take their bodies seriously. I use the term "crisis" loosely, as in an extended illness, minor surgery or even a visit to the storage closet to get out the current season's clothes. Not necessarily a crisis in terms of medical emergency or life-threatening illness, but just enough of a shock to cause us to take stock of our health in light of our more keenly-felt deterioration.

For younger women away from home for the first extended period in their lives, it may be the "freshman fifteen," those extra pounds that creep up on them, with too frequent refills from the cafeteria line or too many late-night pizzas after work or too many hours stagnating in library study carrels.

Or maybe it's a woman's realization a few months after her baby is born that all those cravings for ice cream, so good for the growing fetus, went unnoticed as the fat cushioning the baby became a permanent part of what now seems like a grossly misshapen body.

For some women the shock comes closer to mid-life, when metabolism slows down or blood pressure goes up, even though eating and exercise habits haven't changed dramatically. It's that glance in the mirror and the rude awakening that the reflection is a true one, not the result of poor lighting or diminishing eyesight.

After the first sense of outrage at our recalcitrant bodies that refuse to get back in shape and discomfort in clothes that pinch just a little too tightly, we begin to face a reality that's not often pleasant: Our bodies, if not fragile, are at least mortal, and cry out for attention before we develop serious health problems that might have been controlled.

I'm not talking about the few extra pounds that accumulate over time, so that we have to admit we're not cheerleader or covergirl material. It's not body image, but body health that's the issue. It's about cholesterol clogging arteries, blood pressure that silently soars while we're clueless as to what's happening inside, limp and lifeless hair that signals a deficient diet. Most importantly, it's about listlessness and decreased energy that prevent us from living life to the fullest.

Psychologist Abraham Maslow, famous for his theory of the hierarchy of needs, believed that unless we attend to most basic life requirements, such as food, shelter, security, we can never move to the higher levels of life, where we can enjoy aesthetic pleasures or, at the highest level, attend to God and others. In most textbook illustrations of this theory, it's the impoverished people who can't afford healthy food that we read about. But even among the middle class and the more privileged, something rings true about Maslow's hierarchy. If we're eating, but overeating or eating poorly in the midst of nutritional plenty, have we really moved beyond those lower rungs of the hierarchy? Or do we still need to clean up our health acts before we can be whole enough to move beyond self-absorption?

"Self-actualization"—Maslow's term for the ultimate goal of human development—seems a worthy goal for women. For many of us, overfed and overtired, that journey toward fulfillment might mean backtracking to assess how healthy we really are. Convinced that we've reached the higher rungs—fulfilling self-esteem and aesthetic needs—have we shortchanged our more basic needs? Fast-paced life-styles usually mean fast food, deadening in the fat, cholesterol and sodium they pour into defenseless bodies as we concentrate on feeding our minds or careers. Our modern modes of relaxation (if we even take the time to relax) also take their toll as we lull in front of videos in our living rooms or collapse on the couch to listen to our newest CD after a long ride home from work.

A friend of mine who confronted a real physical crisis, cancer, reawakened in me concern for my own health. Confronted by the ultimate insult to her body, possible death, she began to reassess her own personal and physical goals. Although she'd always been a healthful eater and regular exerciser, now she was even more cautious about what she put into her body and more committed to keeping it in shape.

For many women today, it's not a physical cancer that's the villain but a disease as potentially harmful: a sort of amorphous, nameless eating away of energy and drive. Most of us still have a chance to turn our health around. We can read labels, not just on canned and frozen food at home, but on those fast-food restaurant nutrition guides (in print that sometimes challenges aging eyes) so that we're aware of what we're taking into our bodies. We can choose to eat and drink moderately, even in times of stress. We can walk rather than drive, with friends or spouses or children, or even alone, refreshing our spirits along with our bodies.

And we can do all this not to look sexy in a swimsuit (a

goal I've long ago given up as unrealizable and unwanted) but to make the most of our days, so we can live life on the top rung of Maslow's ladder. Having taken care of our bodily needs, we can pursue higher goals. Healthy in mind and body, we can move beyond those elemental needs with enough energy to make a real difference in the lives of others.

ॐ BEGINNING TODAY... I will take stock of my physical health, assessing what and how much I eat and how much exercise I make room for in my life. I will fine-tune my life, by making healthier choices, so that I will have more energy to devote to the real essentials in my life.

Growing Old With Grace

There was also a prophet, Anna the daughter of Phanuel, of the tribe of Asher. She was of a great age....—Luke 2:36

T his was her day of celebration, and she was being honored by friends for all she had been and done in her lifetime. Nearly seventy, she radiated energy and a passion for living. What grace and graciousness, what self-confidence she exudes, I whispered to a friend as the celebratory prayer service neared its end. Then, as if to dramatize my musings, she glided toward the front of the group and raised high a banner of streamers. Singing the joyful words of the final song, she danced smilingly through the congregation with the banner, light bouncing off her white hair, streamers fluttering over the heads of her friends who basked in her love.

This is how I want to age, I thought. Then with a jolt, I realized I was well along in the aging process. She was nearing the end of the transformation I was already immersed in, one I had not always celebrated but often grumbled about as the problems and pains of the process overshadowed its beauty.

It didn't happen overnight, no obvious borderline marking off youth from middle age. But here I am, squarely situated in those middle years. The physical were the most obvious changes: the graying hair ("Yep, about 50 percent gray," a beautician had informed me matter-of-factly), the pounds harder to shed, my limbs a little stiffer as I rose from bed each morning, the aging spots dotting my hands.

More disturbing, though, were symptoms of an aging mind. Always proud of my grasp of detail, my "mind like a steel trap," as one friend termed it, I found the details slipping away, the steel trap squeaking (like the Tin Man in *The Wizard of Oz*), "Oil me, oil me." Names eluded me, names of people I knew not only casually but had worked with five years previous. Dates and phone numbers, the few items I needed from the grocery store—I could no longer rely on my memory. As long as I remembered the pen and notepad, I realized through trial and error, I'd get through.

A friend a few years older had sounded the warning. "I really thought I was developing Alzheimer's," she said, recounting in retrospect that she had learned some memory loss was part of many women's natural aging. "Get ready to retrace your steps a lot," she advised. I do, much to the amusement of younger friends who see me stopped in the middle of a staircase as I jog my brain into sharing with me why I had headed that way in the first place. Sometimes the answer comes in a flash, other times I just give up.

I've begun to integrate the bodily and mental changes into living, becoming more comfortable with them, compensating as best I can. They're both related to physical aging, of the body and the mind. But how do I cope with, or even forestall, the hardening of the arteries of attitude that subtly intrude as I age? How do I prevent myself from becoming a graceless "old fuddydud" challenged by the "young whippersnappers"? To my surprise, I find myself muttering negative judgments on the visions and schemes of my juniors, still ready to take on the world. Remembering my own youthful optimism, I wonder how I can squelch theirs, even if I don't speak my criticisms aloud. "It won't work, no one will buy it" or "We already tried that years ago" were phrases that had irked me in my youth; now they're insinuating themselves into my mental vocabulary.

The trend scares me. I know that wisdom and experience are part of aging, but I must strike a careful balance between realism and skepticism.

The example of my seventy-ish friend with whom I'm celebrating calls me back to reflect on the progress of my life, to give an accounting of my aging and to take charge of its direction. A few decades from now, will I be as graceful as she is? That's my dream, but it will happen only through daily acceptance of and reflection on my self in transformation. Only then will I be nimble enough, in spirit if not in body, to sing and dance before my friends and

Creator in thanksgiving and celebration of the aging but ageless person I'm striving to become.

❧ BEGINNING TODAY... I will consciously celebrate rather than resist my aging. I will keep my body and mind in shape so their deterioration won't be a detriment to me. But should my efforts fail, I vow to remain young in spirit by staying open to new ideas, by affirming the vision of those working for change, by imitating the aging behaviors of women I admire.

Sports(wo)manship

"For the girls out there who one day want to dream of either being an Olympian or going to college or just competing and knowing that it's OK to go out there and sweat and dive and get dirty...this is that day."
—Lisa Fernandez, pitcher on the 1996 U.S. gold-medal softball team

The sweet smell of sweat. For women, it's also the sweet smell of success.

Breaking down the sweat barrier in a culture that puts such a priority on athletics signals another victory for women who strive to celebrate the totality of their gifts.

Not long ago, opportunities for women's athletics, and sweat, were painfully limited. Even fifteen years ago, if a conversation I had was at all typical. A young woman who wanted to get into shape after the birth of her child informed me that she had signed up for an aerobics class, adding jokingly and somewhat apologetically, "But I don't sweat, I glisten." She felt the need to assure me that even though she would be engaging in strenuous exercise, she would still be a "lady."

In this woman's growing-up years, a young woman might have played volleyball or softball. If she competed seriously, she drew little attention, at least from the public. During that same era, when I taught at a girls' high school, the school's athletic director waged a running letter-writing battle in the daily papers aimed at shaming sports reporters into devoting more, if not yet equal, space to high school and college women's sports. Thankfully, that coverage is expanding. This morning, I picked up a newspaper with a front-page photo of a jubilant girls' high school volleyball team celebrating a fourth consecutive state title. On the front page of the inside sports section, more surprises—color photos of another division girls' volleyball state champion team and a girls' soccer team carrying home a state trophy. In a recent issue of the paper, the lead story and photos in the sports section featured the clash between two local college basketball teams—surprisingly, women's.

Few young women athletes will achieve at the level that warrants newspaper coverage. But what's important is that they're breaking down the barriers to playing and achieving. They will have a chance to know the discipline of practice, the joys and tensions of building a team, the injustice of poor calls by incompetent refs, the graciousness of winning, the lip-biting sadness of putting on a good face to shake hands with the other team after a close defeat.

Why did you play sports growing up, I asked a woman in her mid-twenties. She referred me to an ad by Nike, promoting girls' sports. It reads in part: "If you let me play, I will like myself more. I will have more self-confidence. I will suffer less depression. I will be more likely to leave a man who beats me. I will learn what it means to be strong." In short, my friend told me, "playing sports empowered me. It gave me a sense of achievement and equality."

Even more than learning about competition and victory, young women are building habits into their lives that will allow them to live fully beyond their adolescent years. With positive sports experiences as reminders, they'll seek out an adult recreational softball league in the neighborhood or a coed winter volleyball team in the parish—ways to limber up, stretch out, release energy and build community when the pressures of job or family begin to eat away at them. As my oldest daughter jokingly told me, "Sports let me get out my aggressions so I don't come home and beat up my younger sisters." There's more then a kernel of wisdom in her jest, the promise of an emotional outlet as she confronts stress in the years to come.

This sports habit can also build bridges between generations. A few years ago, young girls were coached by men, usually their fathers, who had grown up playing basketball or baseball, or who were willing to attend soccer clinics to learn the rudiments of this fast-growing sport that their daughters were so eager to try. Now a generation of women has grown up participating rather than merely observing these sports. "Coach," a word that in English has no gender markers, now easily fits either sex as a title of honor and respect. Even if women choose not to play sports as adults, with their knowledge of the rules and strategies and their experience as players, they can teach and be models for the next generation. Such influence was driven home to me last year in a crowded church during an evening funeral. I had come in sadness—a young woman friend had died suddenly from a rare illness—but I left feeling uplifted. Too fragile to play soccer in her later years, my friend had continued to coach young girls. The pews were filled with the future women whose lives she had touched as a soccer coach and as a teacher in the parish religion program. She had helped them, not only spiritually but also physically, begin to mature into healthy women.

Nearly two thousand years ago Saint Paul drew upon the experience of sports as a metaphor for his spiritual struggles: "I have fought the good fight, I have run the race." Although Christians over the ages have been tempted to make the relation between the spirit and the flesh an adversarial one—denying the flesh so the soul can flourish—the two can't really be separated.

A sound mind and a sound spirit—in a sweaty body. It doesn't quite have the lilting rhythms of the ancients' "A sound mind in a sound body," but the wisdom still rings true for modern women in their quest for wholeness.

ॐ BEGINNING TODAY... I will take an inventory of my sports skills to determine how I can best use them to improve myself and to help other women grow. If my skills are nonexistent, I will cheer on others in their enjoyment of sports.

Self-reliance

[Ruth] said, "Please, let me glean and gather among the sheaves behind the reapers." So she came, and she has been on her feet from early this morning until now, without resting even for a moment.—Ruth 2:7

"You can do it!" I encourage a female student, as she visits my office for college scheduling advice. "You can do it, it's all in your head. Other women have done it and will help you through it." But fear radiates from her eyes as she projects years of past failure into the future. I watch her cower in her chair as she writes the course and section number on the schedule.

I feel like grabbing her by the shoulders, looking her in the eyes, and yelling, "Face your fears. You can learn math!" But I restrain myself lest I merely aggravate her feelings of inadequacy.

I've observed it over and over again, women like her abusing themselves by limiting personal growth because of fear. It's far more than a personal history of math inadequacy that burdens her and others like her. It's a cultural mindset that they've bought into, the same one that systematically divides careers and aspirations by gender, displaying them like so many "his" and "hers" hand towels hung out for guests, blue for him, pink for her.

By now we should be beyond these limiting definitions, but we're not. So it takes women with spunk, unconcerned about being labeled "unfeminine," to push back the boulders of ignorance that block the light of understanding. They're out there, but we need to share their stories of breaking down the walls of gender expectations. Better yet, have them share their own and watch as the veils fall from the eyes of listeners.

One woman told some of her story to my students in a speech class. Having recently worked her way back into formal education after a few years in the work force, she came to me at a loss for a topic for an informative speech she had to prepare. "So what have you done in your life that you could talk about?" I quizzed her privately.

What she had done would have blown the minds of younger classmates if she'd had time to tell all. What we finally decided on was a topic of interest to students, most of whom had been late for class because the main road leading to the college seemed constantly under repair but never in good shape. For years this woman had worked on a road crew (one of many out-of-the-ordinary jobs she'd held), so she decided to inform the class about asphalt—what it was and why it broke down so quickly under the midwest's winter weather. In the end, she urged her listeners to be kind to the flaggers who directed carloads of disgruntled, impatient drivers. She knew from personal experience how inconsiderate drivers could be.

The students were impressed, and they learned

something, so she'd definitely achieved the goal of her speech. For sure, they learned about crumbling asphalt—the immediate lesson—but also about pushing personal and cultural limits. Less polished in some academic areas than many of the younger students in the class, the speaker exuded a self-confidence that they could only hope for, not because of her age, but because she had tested and challenged herself.

She is not alone in her willingness to break out of rigid categories. In an old neighborhood of my city, a group of women have been making an impact on their neighbors and on those who adhere rigidly to role definition. They bought an old school building and renovated it into housing for low-income families, many headed by single parents, some too old to afford decent housing on their limited income. The women did what others said couldn't be done; now they're teaching others. The basement of the old school has been transformed into workshops, where women conduct "self-help" clinics on home repairs, initially for women, but increasingly for any group who wants to be more self-sufficient. The classes fill up faster than they can schedule them.

They're teaching more than home repairs. To the residents, who've often been out of the loop of power and systems, they're modeling other skills—organizing groups, working with city agencies, tapping into resources they never knew existed.

Still, this breaking out of boundaries does not come easily. It needs constant affirmation. And some handholding, at first.

A year ago, my student with math anxiety would never have predicted that she could succeed. After hallway conferences where I urged her to get tutoring or boosted her spirits when she flunked tests, she and I can celebrate her success. A few weeks ago, sitting in my office discussing the next semester's schedule, she smiled shyly as she pointed to the math grade on her transcript: "I did it. I got a C."

That she will never love math or excel in it is certain. But math excellence is not the real lesson here, and she seems to know it. A year ago, she had slumped in her chair, defeated before she had even been tried, certain she could never succeed.

Today, she points to that C proudly, a symbol in a sea of A's and B's of her determination to navigate uncharted waters and her willingness to take a few risks.

֍ BEGINNING TODAY... I will examine my life for ways that I buy into cultural stereotypes that inhibit my growth as a whole person. I will affirm any steps other women take to do the same, no matter how insignificant and unpublicized they may be.

Giving...and Holding Back

Each of you must give as you have made up your mind,
not reluctantly or under compulsion, for God loves a
cheerful giver.—2 Corinthians 9:7

Sixteen preteen girls had signed up for neighborhood softball, but their former coach was moving to the fast-pitch league. "We're looking for coaches. If no one volunteers, we won't have a team," the girls' softball commissioner explained over the phone, asking if I'd take the job.

"Sorry, I can't. Good luck!" was my spontaneous and guiltless reply.

Actually, saying "no" hadn't taken much thought, since I had never played on a softball team. Even after sitting on the sidelines for many seasons of my girls' games, I still hadn't figured out the infield fly rule.

Other requests were tougher to turn down: to lead a Brownie troop (three times, I pat myself on the back, I've said "no" to that job, one that my twelve years in scouts kept pushing me to take), to serve on a search committee for a new hire at work, or to coordinate a parish event. If I had volunteered, it wouldn't have been because I was "under compulsion," as Paul warned the Corinthians. Often my volunteer decisions were made out of my own compulsions.

It's a delicate balance: helping others because Christ calls me to serve, and knowing when to say "no" because I'm not a spring-fed reservoir of ideas, energy and time. Observing others' responses to calls for service has helped me name my own compulsions.

Years ago, as I sat in a circle of first-grade mothers being recruited for Brownie leader, I almost gasped aloud as I noticed one woman grimacing under the pressure of the decision to volunteer. Her tentative inquiries about whether the girls could hold nighttime meetings and how many training sessions she'd have to attend sent a shiver of familiarity through me. I'd teetered on the edge myself a few times. How could she even consider it, I mused; she's mother to two children, works a full-time job and travels several times a week to an out-of-town university to complete her degree. Luckily for her, someone else volunteered.

But we shouldn't have to be rescued from such dilemmas by someone else's decisions. Once, in a situation much like the scout mother circle, I had put my name on a ballot for a year-long volunteer leadership position at work. Knowing my other commitments—of family and work—my department head berated me for my generosity. "Well, maybe I'll lose," I smiled meekly. But I didn't. And I began to ponder my skewed version of God's will, where I place my fate in the hands of job-distributing God ("if it's meant to be, I'll be elected") rather than making the tough decision not to volunteer in the first place.

The other candidate who had placed her name on the ballot when the organization seemed doomed to extinction was also a woman. What's going on here, I wondered as I looked around to see who was filling the significant roles, all volunteer positions. The answer was all too obvious: women.

"Sometimes the best man for a job is a woman." I used to chuckle at the cleverness of the slogan, proud that women's talents were beginning to be appreciated. But now

I think we took that clever play on words too seriously. Sometimes the best man might actually be a man, especially if women are losing control of their schedules and their selves because they're spread too thin. Saint Paul would have urged us to be useful to others in need, but some of us have allowed "useful" to degenerate into "used," rendering us ultimately "useless" to ourselves and to those who count on our wholeness.

Is it because we view ourselves as nurturers that we continue to give and give beyond the point of physical and emotional health? Even though we're already full-time mothers or our careers make as many demands on our time as men's do, why do we eke out extra hours a week to pitch in when the distress flags go up, but men seem able to face their limitations more sanely and just say no?

"It is in giving that we receive," the familiar prayer of Saint Francis reminds us. But when we give out of compulsion, when we give from wells that have run dry, the benefits to ourselves and others are of dubious worth. Receiving from others is also a virtue, allowing others the gift of giving to us.

৯ BEGINNING TODAY... When I am asked to take on another responsibility, before I give my response I will take time to reflect on the wisdom of accepting. I will try to understand why I am saying "yes." Will I be merely serving some unfulfilled need I have or will I truly be serving others? I will consider whether saying "no" will be more beneficial to myself and those I've already committed my talents to. If I do accept, I will embrace my new role wholeheartedly.

Pressure to Marry

*Therefore a man leaves his father and his mother and
clings to his wife, and they become one flesh.*
—Genesis 2:24

T he question, in more or less subtle variations, hovers
over office water coolers, among mourners at funeral
parlors and, most blatantly, on the dance floor at
wedding receptions whenever an unescorted woman
arrives: "What's a nice girl like her doing still single?" Often
the unspoken implication is crueler: "What's wrong with
her that she hasn't found a man?"

Spoken or not, it's in the not-so-covert glance at her left
hand or the whisking her off to meet "a guy you'll really
like." Though well-meaning, these efforts to attach every
woman to a man degrade all women, since they point to the
same conclusion: Without a man you're less than whole.

Though married, I'm insulted by the assumptions of this
definition of woman: that she is incapable of managing the
day-to-day demands of life without a male to guide her, that
without sexual intimacy she can't be intimate, that deep
friendships between women are not as life-giving as those in
marriage, or, even worse, less than natural.

Smug in my own rich married relationship, I often
forget that marriage may not be the goal for all women,
especially those who are secure in their identities as
individuals. A recent comment from an unmarried woman
at first insulted then startled me, recapturing for me a
mindset that I had put aside after marriage. Commenting on
the pain a mutual friend was experiencing with a romance

gone sour, she said, in the outspoken manner I have grown used to: "I don't even know why she'd want to get married. Most of my married friends envy my life." Only she could have thrown off the comment so directly, without casting judgment on me and my choice in life.

Taken aback, I was transported to premarriage days twenty years earlier, when I had struggled with the decision to marry. Confident in my career and my friendships, I feared moving into a permanent commitment with a man if it meant I'd have to give up my independence and my personality. Unfortunately, I'd seen too many marriages where the woman's identity had been submerged by the man's, so that she was no longer "person" or "woman" but only "wife."

A bit uncomfortable with my friend's generalization about unhappy marriages, I tried to envision how single women might see me: Who was really in the cage? Was I the zoo visitor or the animal behind the bars? Often the object of society's pity, perhaps my single friends were pitying me for what they considered my restricted life.

There are some pretty distorted assumptions floating around our culture that often victimize single and married women: that the Sacrament of Matrimony guarantees an intimacy and friendship which all married women enjoy; that remaining in a loveless, stifling marriage is preferable to going it alone; that women who lose their mates to death will never again find happiness or fulfillment.

But real women's lives defy these absurd implications. The grace and strength with which my single friends absorb others' faulty judgments, dismissing them as irrelevant and getting on with the business of living, inspires all women to reexamine essential values. What matters are matters of the soul, the core of the woman: whether she loves and whether she is loved. All else is peripheral.

Loving is loving—whether the object of affection is my child or my single friend's godchild. Giving is giving— whether it's my gift to my spouse or my single friend's homemade noodles or pie shared at a birthday celebration. And the same goes for showing affection, nurturing and feeling others' pain; it's the state of mind and heart that counts, not the state in life.

As a married woman I sometimes hide behind the excuse of a family and children when I'm challenged to reach out to the world beyond them. Too often guilty of self-absorption, I am challenged to be more generous and selfless by the example of my single friends who open not only their purses, but also their eyes and hearts, to those in need.

Each of us—as single woman, married woman, vowed religious—has her own way of manifesting love and of being for others. To make choices, major ones like state of life or minor ones as we live it, then to be at peace with those choices—that is what all women are called to by God, that is the meaning of vocation.

❧ BEGINNING TODAY... I will reevaluate my behavior or words to and about women who have chosen a different vocation in life. Do I judge them as inferior merely because their lives are different? If the judgment has been unintentional, I will try to avoid this frame of mind in the future. If I know I have offended other women, I will curb my words or apologize to them for my insensitivity.

Woman as Mother

In short, Mrs. Pontellier was not a mother-woman....
They were women who idolized their children, worshiped
their husbands, and esteemed it a holy privilege to efface
themselves as individuals and grow wings as ministering
angels.—Kate Chopin, The Awakening

For many in our culture, "woman" is synonymous with "mother." If you're one, you're automatically the other. If you're comfortable as woman, you'll glide smoothly into your role as mother. And surely if you're a wife you'll be a mother, or your life will be incomplete.

But motherhood isn't a goal or a possibility for all women. Those who never bear children often bear the psychological and social pressures imposed by parents, friends, coworkers, who though usually well-intentioned, urge them to move into motherhood before they're ready or imply that their childless state reflects their inadequacy.

Marrying at almost thirty, I would smile good-naturedly at my mother-in-law's occasional quip that her "grandmother gland was going to dry up soon." She wasn't really pressuring me, I realized as I stepped away to objectively appreciate her jest; this was her way of voicing her own desire for the riches of grandparenting that her friends were already enjoying. She would be a wonderful grandmother and our children would be blessed with the affection she would shower on them. Someday, but not yet, I vowed in early marriage. I had just moved into a relationship with all its newness and adjustments; God willing, babies would come...later. And they did.

But others who hope for children "sooner or later" are not so blessed in seeing their dreams take flesh. I watch the pain of friends who ache for children but can't conceive or whose pregnancies end in miscarriage. Doctor after doctor, test after test followed by surgeries to remedy the diagnosed problems, and still no success. Some women pursue at great cost their goal of giving birth to children, suffering the embarrassment and discomfort of medical procedures whose success rate is sometimes dubious and expense is great. Others, resigned to the fact that children will never be a part of their lives, move on to strengthening their relation with the man who has shared in a dream denied, or to nurturing children other than their own. I have witnessed quiet pain tingeing their joy at the announcement of a friend's pregnancy and have admired their strength as they wrap one more gift for another baby shower at which they're not the guest of honor.

But motherhood achieved doesn't necessarily end the pressure on women to conform to some vaguely defined image of "mother-woman." Conceiving and bearing a child may be the easy part; after that there are even higher expectations to meet.

"Don't tell me your children fight," an unmarried sister once teased me as I explained my plan to spend more time at home during the summer to fend off quarrels among my three children, though they were old enough to be home alone. My sister's feigned horror at the idea of fighting among the Barkley girls, "perfect" as they were to the eyes of outsiders, was her parody on the cultural expectations of mothers.

Society perpetuates this archetypal vision of "the good mother" based on unrealizable standards, and mothers continue to be molded by it, nebulous though it is. We know by what ages our children should walk and talk and how they should behave in restaurants, stores and church. By their behavior, we are judged not only as mothers but as women. Holding ourselves to an impossible goal, we allow our self-concepts to wither with every critical comment from adults about our child-rearing or every complaint from our children about our mothering.

We seem to have forgotten that motherhood is a vocation, one that not every woman feels called to or accepts willingly. Some hear the call but are unable to act upon it; others live mother-lives fraught with frustration because they find little support when their best efforts are deemed failures in the eyes of critics who have never known, or perhaps have forgotten, how demanding motherhood can be, how some days are survived only through prayer and God's grace.

Whether childless by choice or genetics, whether mother to one or many, women need to assert their multidimensionality. They need reminders and affirmations that allow them to believe that their lives are fuller than this limiting description of them as women-mothers. Their mothering (or lack of it) should not be the sole standard by which their woman-worth is measured.

₰ BEGINNING TODAY... I will break out of (or help others break out of) the confining definition of woman as primarily child-bearer and rearer. If I am a mother of young children, I will read a magazine or watch a television show geared to adults—without my children—and relish my individuality. If I am a woman with no children living with me, I will plan an activity with a woman with children and set one rule for the outing: no talk about children.

The Name Game

O, be some other name!
What's in a name? That which we call a rose
By any other word would smell as sweet.
—*William Shakespeare,* Romeo and Juliet

For being mere symbols, words can cause a lot of trouble. Especially names. Especially for women.

Even on the simplest level, words and names are more complicated than they seem, because of what they symbolize. Titles, for instance. Is it Ms., Miss, Mrs., Rev. or Dr.? Granted, words are not the reality, but they help determine how we perceive reality. Even small words, seemingly insignificant words, can blur or sharpen the image of people we meet.

Ms., for instance. A relatively new linguistic tag, a combination of Miss and Mrs., this tiny word does a great service to our language, so poverty-stricken in areas of family relations. Like a great compromiser and a leveler, the equivalent of the male Mr., it's a label that avoids markers of marital status. Though it's been around long enough to gain respect and usage in the media, some still resist it ("too feminist"), and inequality persists, the man allowed to be an individual, a person in his own right, while a woman's marital status, through Mrs. or Miss, becomes part of the public domain.

On the professional level, women can be subtly dismissed because of a label, or the absence of one. In a women's discussion group, I heard a young colleague empathize with one of her senior academic leaders about an incident that seemed at first minor when I heard her relate it; only as I reflected on it did I understand the younger woman's justified distress. At a meeting of college personnel, everyone but her senior friend had been introduced by academic titles, usually "doctor"; throughout the evening she had been referred to by her first name. So what, was my first reaction, she's warm and accessible; people feel comfortable addressing her on a first-name basis. Not one to make a fuss about formalities, she had not pushed the issue, but her young colleague had. And rightly so, I now see. She had worked hard for her Ph.D., and if others were being identified by theirs, she had the same right to public respect.

We deserve to be called by names we feel at home with, names that reflect who we are. That principle, however, does little to resolve the dilemma of in-law names, one of the most slippery issues a newly married woman has to face. I have known few women who have dealt with this successfully, unless the mother-in-law graciously gives in or unless she has no strong feelings about what her daughter-in-law should call her in their new relationship. One young friend says she takes lots of teasing from her husband's sisters about her awkwardness in addressing his mother. Since she and her husband had been friends for many years before marriage, she had grown up calling her "Mrs."; she's uncomfortable suddenly switching to her first name or to the favorite of many mothers-in-law, "Mom."

"Such dilemmas of marriage," she tells me. "I mean I care about her, but I already have a mom."

Of course, she's the same newlywed who'd already faced head-on another sticky name issue: whether to keep her family name or adopt her husband's. For some women, the issue is easily resolved: Adopting the husband's name is merely a cultural convention that says little about the true relation between husband and wife. He can keep his name, I'll keep mine, is their simple solution.

Not so simple for some women, depending on their context. One friend tried that approach in a small rural community and met criticism and some hostility. If you love your husband, why aren't you proud to wear his name, her social work clients wondered skeptically.

My young friend's solution was more typical: a hyphenated surname that combined the two family names. At least she thought it would be more acceptable, until her husband's family raised eyebrows at the decision. And these folks had been around long enough that they should have been used to such compromises. They're still adapting; she's holding firm.

Her blended name has a nice ring to it, and fits easily with many other combinations, according to her toddler niece, her sister's daughter. The niece likes the hyphenated name so much that she appends it to the first names of everyone in the family: my friend's husband, brother-in-law, even the couple's puppy. Her in-laws are not amused.

But the child stands by her labels, careless and unconcerned about violating customs, arbitrary as they are, that many people hold dear. There's an innocence in her that allows her to see clearly what many of her elders are blinded to.

Years ago, mothering my young children, I broke out a deck of playing cards, shuffled them and began instructing my five-year-old daughter in a new game. I dealt the prescribed number of cards, then consulted the directions. "The first player takes a card from the player on his right," I read aloud. "They mean her right," she corrected me, as if someone had made an incredibly stupid error. The very young in their wisdom have little use for generic interpretations of masculine pronouns.

"What's in a name?" the young Juliet pined as she sought to work out her love affair with Romeo, who wore the dreaded name Montague, enemies to her own Capulet clan. "O, be some other name," she urged him, just as women are urged today by those who believe they'd "smell as sweet," no matter what they're called. But they wouldn't. Names, though not reality, reflect and shape reality. And for a woman, that reality is often an individuality she has worked too hard to establish to simply throw away for the sake of an arbitrary and unexamined cultural convention.

❧ BEGINNING TODAY... I will be sensitive to other women's feelings about their names: first names, family names and titles. I will not impose my own name-values on them, whether I think theirs too old-fashioned or too liberal. By respecting their names, I will show that I revere them for their uniqueness as women.

Women and Church

*I pity the man that has no higher views of woman's
nature and duty and influence than to put her under foot,
and then endeavor to sanctify the meanness of the act by
pleading for it the sanction of religion.—1860 sermon by
Rev. A. P. Mead*

This was my first bat mitzvah, the Jewish celebration
of a young girl's coming of age in her faith. At
thirteen, my friends' daughter moved with
confidence toward the front of the synagogue, where she
demonstrated to the congregation knowledge of her faith
and the Scriptures. For months she had studied under a
young woman rabbinical student, learning Hebrew and
breaking open a passage of Scripture. This morning she
confidently read in Hebrew as family members translated
for those of us who had no knowledge of the ancient
language. Taking the microphone as the rabbis nodded
approvingly, she shared her insights on the biblical passage
she had read, reminding us that God was calling us to use
our talents and wealth to help the less fortunate. We heard
praise from a rabbi about her efforts to put her
understanding of that passage into practice at a local
hospital. In a final dramatic ritual, the young girl helped
unveil the Torah, the most sacred of books, and carried it
high as she processed among the congregation.

Thirteen, I mused with wonder and disappointment,
wonder at the teen and her faith, disappointment in myself
for being so deluded about the progressiveness of my own
religion. Here is a child, a girl-child at that, preaching and

teaching in the temple as Jesus had once done. My mind rewound tapes of the Holy Saturday service at my Catholic parish a few weeks earlier. That holy night full of ritual and celebration, the culmination of weeks of Lenten fasting and prayer, had been filled with as much pain for me as the bat mitzvah had been with joy for this young woman.

Until that Holy Saturday, I had grasped on an intellectual level the ever-present gap between men and women in the practice of my religion. But that night, perhaps because the symbolic service invited an emotional response, I felt an intense pain at the marginal role women played in my Church.

Once the lights in the church had been extinguished, the congregation was invited out into the cold around a roaring bonfire lighting the night. In the midnight quiet broken only by occasional prayers and *a cappella* chant, the procession moved through the crowd for the blessing of the fire and the lighting of the paschal candle that would burn in our church sanctuary. In flowing vestments at the center of the ceremony were the priest, several deacons and teenage servers, altar boys to be precise. Not a woman in sight, except on the outskirts of the crowd. What a way to start the Church year, I fumed, angry at myself for tolerating such an exclusive ceremony. This night of light had become a night of gloom and darkness for me.

For the rest of the Mass, I fought off negative emotions that kept intruding on my prayer. Christ had died for all of us. This was my Church as much as a man's Church. I consoled myself by noticing that the choir director and a few readers were women, but the altar overflowing with men did little to comfort me.

So weeks later, the bat mitzvah, though a cause for

rejoicing at a young woman's stature in her faith, became a painful reminder of how far my own had yet to come. I was growing weary of the rhetoric about the historic basis for women's role in the Church. Never before had I understood the anger of some friends who for years had worked for more equality for women. My eyes opened through a Jewish ceremony, I realized that the ancient faith of the Old Testament had somehow overcome the historical precedents of woman's role, its believers realizing that religion must adapt to changing cultures. Their faith must grow or it was doomed to die. Why couldn't we, of the New Testament, fill old wineskins with twentieth-century wine?

From conversations with friends practicing their Catholic faith in parishes often viewed with suspicion by the hierarchy, I see glimmers of hope, the result of dialogue and action among faith-full women and men. Tired of fighting for Church positions deemed historically acceptable to ordained men only, they're working for women's entry into positions with less formal authority but more potential for leadership. Rather than being disillusioned, they've channeled their energies into positive outlets where they see possibilities for change.

And they're keeping their struggle in perspective, inspired by even the smallest of changes, especially those coming from the people in the pew. At a Christmas open house, I listened to a male friend (a member of a less-than-mainstream parish) share with others his "epiphany" moment of the past week. On their way back from a ride among rural towns to cut down a Christmas tree for their urban home, he and his wife had stopped over in a small town, the darkened streets lined with brilliant luminaries, tiny candles in sand-filled paper sacks. Last year my friends had admired the brilliance of the candle-lit streets, but this year they wanted to view firsthand the live nativity scene at the center of town.

With glee in his voice, my friend, who was often weary of his Church's foot-dragging on women's issues, noted one symbolic detail: This town's baby Jesus had been a baby girl, wrapped in pink. He knew, of course, that one rural creche scene does not represent Church thinking, but he took great delight in this ground-level subversion of the oldest argument against women's leadership in the Church: that Jesus had been a man and had chosen men as his apostles.

This story was an unexpected Christmas gift for me, helping me continue to deal with my anger at issues of inequity. I was recharged by this Christmas anecdote, pondering the enlightened vision of these real people in a real town who in their simplicity had broken through the darkness of a centuries-old mindset. Those small-town streets had been flooded with light in more ways than one.

ﻭ BEGINNING TODAY... I will gently but firmly work for more equality for women in Church leadership, by affirming male and female leaders who promote women and their talents and by urging women to move into positions where they can use their gifts to help others grow in their faith.

The Work of Tears

*[God] will wipe every tear from their eyes. Death will be
no more; mourning and crying and pain will be no
more.*—Revelation 21:4

I should call her back now, I think, as I listen to my
sister's message on the phone answering machine. I
should, but I can't. I need to, but I can't.

I can't, because if I call her, I know the concern in her
voice, her empathy with my own pain will lead inevitably
to the one thing I don't want right now—tears. Right now I
just don't have the time or the energy for what I know I
need most, a good cry.

But I do call, and we talk briefly, skirting around the
edges of our mutual concern. As I hear the tremor begin in
my voice (oh, she hears it too, I'm certain, but she isn't one
to push), I find an excuse to cut the conversation short and
get on with being productive in my work.

But the real work is left undone for the moment, the
work that only tears can do.

It's messy work, get-down-to-the-bottom-of-things

work. Once tears start, it's hard to slow them down, and it's not easy to predict when they'll end. That's why I'm cautious about letting them begin. I'm not comfortable being out of control, or in the control of tears, especially when there are people to meet, appearances to keep up. And swollen eyes don't disappear quickly, even overnight. They're a dead giveaway to even the most casual observer that something is awry. They're often unsettling, especially to those who haven't experienced their healing power.

I have seen men cry—at the death of a parent or the death of a relationship or the trauma of an accident—but tears are still largely the domain of women, at least in our culture. I worry that in women's move toward equality, especially in the work force, we risk giving them up, buying into the pop song mentality that says "Big girls don't cry."

But big girls do, as we should.

Why should the renewing power of tears be the privilege of the young? Babies know how to cry, unaware of cultural censures about time, place or volume. I've heard some inspiringly therapeutic wailing from infants and toddlers that struck a chord within me. "I know just how you feel," I say to myself as I listen, less annoyed than envious, wishing I were as unconcerned as they about how my crying would be received.

As girls grow, even as preteens, they assimilate the belief that crying is a sign of weakness. "Crybaby" is a stinging taunt no one likes to have hurled at her. So girls learn to suppress tears for fear of embarrassment, unaware that their ability to cry might be an index of their emotional maturity rather than immaturity.

Sometimes it takes friends to give not-so-little girls permission to cry. Recently, one of my college students who had missed an exam because she had to leave town suddenly for her grandfather's funeral, met me to arrange makeup work.

"So, how are you doing?" I asked her as she sat down, and I noted her effort to concentrate on material that I knew was far removed from what was most on her mind.

"I'm OK now," she smiled, telling me how touched she had been when a carload of her dorm friends had surprised her by attending her grandfather's wake. It was their presence as well as their question that had helped her through it. Had she cried, they wondered, reminding her she didn't have to be so "strong." They knew from having met her grandfather when he'd visited her on campus what a bond they'd had.

"So, have you cried?" I asked.

"I was doing OK until they played 'Taps' at the cemetery," an honor due her grandfather because of his military service. "Then I lost it and could hardly stop."

She said this without apology. Her friends had known and she had known that closure to this life of love could not begin until the tears flowed. Her tears had been unexpected—precipitated by the mournful and symbolic notes of a lone bugle—but she welcomed them as long overdue.

That's how it is with tears: The more we resist them, the more we need them.

A sign of weakness, some might say, chalking them up as a "girl thing." But in reality they're the beginning of strength. Whatever seeds have been germinating in the heart—anger, fear, pain—need to be unearthed and examined.

Only as the tears flow, only as the surface, crusted over

from years of repression, loosens up, can the uprooting and heart-healing begin.

&❧ BEGINNING TODAY... I will be sensitive to the quiver in the voice or the sadness in the eyes of friends who need to cry. I will take the time to help them loosen up and let the tears flow so the work of healing can begin.

Losing Control

It was good to have everything clean and folded away, with the hair brushes and tonic bottles sitting straight on the white embroidered linen....—Katherine Anne Porter, "The Jilting of Granny Weatherall"

The previous weeks couldn't have been more hectic. There were interviews for positions recently vacated. A major project involving a dozen colleagues neared completion, but pieces needed to be tidied up before it could be submitted for approval. Her staff had pulled together to help her wrap things up, but loose ends needed tucking in before anyone could relax. To accomplish their goals, all of them would have to stick to the plan mapped out for the next few weeks.

Suddenly the map disintegrated before their eyes.

Surgery—now! That was the doctor's judgment if one hoped to halt the quick-growing cancer identified in the biopsy.

So the plans she had so carefully formulated threatened to explode into near chaos. She'd have to turn over the reins to others, no less dedicated, but less schooled in the bigger picture of their work.

No one blamed it on God, but the timing of the sudden surgery, in the midst of Holy Week, opened itself to reflection—most obviously on suffering, but also on redemption.

It could have been I, not only in this instance with the sudden surgery, but in other cases too similar for comfort, like the situation of an older friend rushed to the emergency room with heart problems.

"I'm not sure how this will affect me," he had shared a week later when he returned, reflecting on his Easter night visit to the ER and his Easter week stay in the cardiac care unit. "But I know it will make a difference in my life."

Both emergencies arose in the context of Holy Week and Easter Week. Both were loaded with symbolism for me, not about my friends' sin and weakness, but about mine, and my need for redemption.

As I mentally recite the major sins I memorized in my catechism days—pride, covetousness, lust, anger, gluttony, envy, sloth—I have little doubt which is mine. From the earliest Church writers through Dante and modern fable-writers, pride has been the fascinating one—most subtle, least obvious to outsiders, but the most damaging. Even earlier, the Greeks had a name for it: *hubris*, an arrogance that admitted no need for the gods.

Today's hubris or pride takes a slightly different shape,

but it's a creature of the same genre. We need to be in control. If we plan out our lives carefully, keep appointment books that mark off our days in fifteen-minute segments, rise early enough to start each day with a "to do" list, rip off one page a day from inspirational calendars for women and integrate the pithy quotes into our day, we will be on top of life. Our three-year plans, our career goals will help us negotiate the messier parts of life.

Such a worldview leaves no room for the unexpected, for the setbacks that are sure to bring the seemingly well-oiled machine of our lives to a screeching halt.

But it's in the setbacks that I come to see my need for God and for others. When confronted with glitches in my personal master plan, I realize control is an illusion. Order in itself is no sin—the straightened desk, the well-run meeting, the task completed on time—but neither is it a virtue, as I'd mistakenly come to believe. Being in control brings a false security, the belief that I'm running the show that can't go on without me.

But, as my friends' Easter surprises taught me, the show does go on. Others step in to teach the class, run the meeting, plan the big event, accept the applause for jobs well done. Stripped of control, my friends gave themselves over to the unpredictability of their lives, day by day coping with each unexpected twist, and emerging graciously from their ordeals, at peace.

Their Easter struggles give new life to me as I grapple with my own hubris, my need to run the world, as I contemplate the void in my life that lack of control would bring. Like my wise friends, role models not only in their careers but in their faith lives, I need to welcome the unexpected into my life.

After all, I've come to realize, it was in the surprise of the unlooked-for empty tomb on Easter morning that the waiting women found their redemption.

᪥ BEGINNING TODAY... I will examine my values and priorities to determine whether I am obsessed with "having everything clean and folded away" and "sitting straight" in my life. I will try to let go of some insignificant points of order in my day. If big plans cave in, I will accept the lack of order as a reminder of my dependence on a higher order in my life.

The Pain of Children

Meanwhile, standing near the cross of Jesus were his mother, and his mother's sister, Mary the wife of Clopas, and Mary Magdalene.—John 19:25

The Gospels, so rich in detail about wedding parties where water miraculously becomes wine, fishing expeditions where nets burst with the day's catch, and campouts and transfigurations on mountains, tell us little about Mary and her life as mother to probably the most celebrated child in history.

An angel's announcement to Joseph about his wife's

pregnancy, Mary's "fiat," word of a census, and, *voilà*, the baby is born, awaiting the visit of shepherds and kings. But something's missing in this account.

Every mother recognizes the obvious gaps in the story of the birth and subsequent voids in the story of Mary and her child. Mothers can complete the story by reflecting on their own mothering, recalling the details with perfect clarity.

The waiting, the debilitating weariness of the first trimester, the anxiety about the baby's health, the first pangs of labor ("How will I know I'm in labor?" a friend asks. "Oh, don't worry," I reply, "you'll know."). Then the birth itself, with an intensity that one unused to childbirth could never begin to imagine. That physical pain, though never forgotten, gets tucked away, stored in a memory drawer rarely opened because it's over and there's no undoing the past.

But the pain never goes away, it's merely transformed. The first bout with colic, the first tooth inching through swollen gums, the first gash in the head that introduces us to the trauma of the emergency room, the first bee sting— the pain, though not really ours, helps us understand our own parents' "It hurts me more than it hurts you."

A few years later, growing used to our toddler's scars and scabs and bruises, we experience a more profound level of pain. "They won't play with me," our child sobs, or "They never even noticed me, all they wanted to talk about was the baby" or "How come she gets birthday cards from him and I don't?"

And later, the pain of stinging words, dashed off in an instant but cutting deeply—about height, weight, complexion, grades, athletic ability. What comfort can a mother give? To strike back with more cutting words, to berate the one who berates, only compounds the ugliness floating around for my child to breathe. A hug, reassurance that the words aren't true, that the speaker didn't really mean them—all the while crying silently in sympathy with a hurting child.

"Mary treasured all these things in her heart"—our only glimpse into the growing-up years between her child's birth and death. What else could the evangelist write? We see her at a wedding, proud of her son's growing prominence and the grace with which he manages the water-to-wine transformation that salvages an awkward situation. But what else is in her heart—when he is brought before the courts to be humiliated and scourged, as he falls along the way toward his death, as he cries out "Abba!" on the cross?

Every mother has been there: wanting to forestall a child's life decisions she knows will end up in misery, but letting go so the child can grow; constantly checking herself and her motherly impulses so she doesn't overstep her bounds, even though she's sure her child will suffer.

Even in their adult-children's years, mothers suffer with their children; they're still our "kids," no matter how we try to release them. Every personal disappointment, every setback in a career, every medical crisis—the pain may really be her offspring's but it's the mother's vicariously.

It seems almost heretical to speak of children and pain in the same breath, accustomed as we are to the sanctified and sanitized images of motherhood in ads: madonna-like mother and child bonding in the newly refurbished labor and delivery room, cuddling under a Christmas tree, frolicking with the dog in the park, embracing at college graduation. To be sure, there are a multitude of warm moments in mothering, but acknowledging only the joy presents an unreal image; we cannot ignore its sorrows.

At our children's birth, we thought we knew what pain was all about. But it's the little deaths along the way, with pain that we could never have predicted, that test our faith. For generations, like the mother of him who endured pain for all our sakes, mothers before us have kept all these things in their hearts, knowing that mothering, with all its blessings, has a downside, one that makes this calling such a bittersweet encounter with the mystery of a creative God.

❧ BEGINNING TODAY... I will savor the joyful moments with my children, no matter what their age. But I will also embrace the pain of motherhood, not with bitterness but with a gratitude that acknowledges that the fullness of this mother-child bond can be experienced only when we face it realistically. I will ask God to bless all mothers with patience and courage as they accept the up and down times in their lives.

Illness and Suffering

*I've just realized what is meant by "grace."—Albert
Camus,* The Plague

She was a beautiful woman, physically and spiritually.
She had battled cancer once and won, and had
remained serene through the turmoil of divorce. We
rejoiced with her at her remarriage and the birth of her
daughter. Not of my religion, she had reenergized my faith
as she refused to be leveled by what for others would have
been one obstacle too many.

Her joy at another pregnancy, at an age when most
women would have shuddered at the thought of the energy
demanded to raise a newborn, then a toddler, then a teen,
caught me by surprise. But she loved life and wanted to
cherish yet another new one. Though I could not imagine
myself facing the same challenge, in my heart I cheered her
on. Her decisions prompted me to revisit my own
commitment to life and living.

A pre-Christmas phone call about her caught me off
guard as I heard the dreaded words "brain tumor." Not her,
not now. Where was the loving God who had guided and
sustained her through crisis after crisis, the faithful God
who had come through with healing, thus upholding me
and my faith by her earlier rescue from cancer?

My Christmas was a somber one as I pondered her
future and the health of her unborn child. Frequent updates
from friends did little to lift my spirits as they reported the
success of the surgery, her struggles in intensive care, her
future of rehabilitation, doubts about her unborn baby's

health that seemed dubious at best.

My sadness was dampening the holiday spirits of my family. In the midst of activity—shopping for last-minute gifts or trudging through muddy fields for the perfect tree— I was able to avoid confronting my wavering faith. But whenever my mind and spirit were undistracted, my moods turned dark, even bitter. It was my teenager who was most tuned into my sobriety, glancing at me in concern as tears welled into my eyes or as uncharacteristic silence crept over me on long car rides that normally provided time for mother-daughter bonding. "What's wrong?" she'd ask with concern.

"What's wrong?" That was the key. On the surface, "what's wrong" seemed to be the miserable hand that was being dealt my God-faithful friend by an unfaithful God. "What's wrong" was all too obvious to me. It was God who had to wake up to what was fair and what to me seemed unfitting, even downright unjust, events I could not reconcile with my image of a providential creator and sustainer of life.

"What's wrong" was the same problem that had troubled all the writers I had taught so convincingly in my college literature classes: how to deal with suffering and still believe in a loving God. I knew the options: reject God for an impersonal fate that would not admit of free will, despair and become more and more cynical with age or take a leap of faith. But academic theorizing about themes and authors' worldviews seemed irrelevant now in my very personal confrontation with suffering; this crisis was something book learning couldn't solve.

The news of the death of the unborn child reached me even as I was grieving aloud with other women about our friend's suffering now and the sufferings of the future. Stunned, we made feeble attempts to console one another that "perhaps this is for the best." But in the face of such mystery, only silence was appropriate.

Given the struggle of the previous weeks and my constant ruminations over the mystery of suffering at a time of year when we least like to confront questions of such depth, I had expected to feel anger at the news, but instead I felt a growing peace as my inner turmoil washed away in the quiet. This ultimate blow to this strong woman, who most likely was herself grappling with God, had forced me to confront "what's wrong?" I knew the futility of trying to figure it all out, of placing suffering within a rational framework.

Either I believed or I didn't. Either I was God or I was a woman trying to find God in the events of my life.

Faced with the either-or-ness of the event, I chose the belief offered to me.

I watch others, especially younger women, struggle to come to grips with death and suffering in their lives and the lives of their friends. Like me, they must make choices about how to confront the unexplainable and unsolvable mysteries that await them as they grow older.

Having faced one loss, then another, thinking I have put my struggle to rest, I know that I will be forced to choose again and again as I come face-to-face with the seemingly meaningless, yet, I trust, ultimately redeeming mystery of suffering in my own and others' lives.

&❧ BEGINNING TODAY... I will reflect on the suffering and evil I encounter in my life and the lives of my friends. Knowing that I most often cannot control it, I will take small steps to alleviate others' pain and help them find a small measure of peace in what may seem like meaningless suffering.

Aging Parents

Honor your father and your mother, so that your days may be long in the land that the Lord our God is giving you.—Exodus 20, 12

"Middle age sure is a bummer!" a fifty-ish friend complained to me. She wasn't moaning about her expanding waistline or her graying hair, or even the endless car trips to shuttle her teenagers around town. What was depressing her was the discomforting role change she was experiencing as her parents moved into old age.

From our total dependence on them in infancy, through our adventuresome toddler years and our storms of adolescence, our parents had faithfully nourished and nurtured us. By whatever name we called them—Mommy and Daddy, Mom and Dad, Mother and Father—both or one of them had been there when we needed them. Now it is evident that they need us.

It's not easy to see our parents slow down—walking

less nimbly, gasping shallowly as they mount a short flight of stairs, catching fewer words of a conversation at a noisy gathering. Weren't they the ones who applauded our own first wobbly steps, who trekked up and down stairs to retrieve us when as toddlers we crawled up stairs but couldn't figure out how to get back down, who rejoiced at our first inarticulate words, who stayed up past midnight to drive our friends home from school dances?

Our parents' physical waning we can take in stride if we reconcile ourselves to the reality of the aging process. It happens, we reason. Bodies can't last forever. Joints begin to stiffen and ache, hair thins and grays, eyes wear out from years of strain.

But it's the mental and emotional changes about our parents that we resist. Always there to dispense advice— about working out differences with siblings, repairing a car, renting an apartment—our parents now surprise us when they seek advice from us about physicians, housing and wills. Or, even more shattering to us as they deteriorate, we give advice and soon they seek it again, unaware that the issues we discussed so recently had ever been raised.

Parenting our parents, a friend's aging mother reminds me, means walking a fine line, knowing when to force the role reversal and when to sit still and wait to be needed. How will we know when we're helping or intruding? Whether to take the car keys away to protect her or allow her the independence of her final days? Whether to put his name on the waiting list of the city's best nursing home or wait for him to decide where and how to manage in old age?

A chatty phone call from an older friend lets me vicariously experience some of the turmoil she's working through as she tries to integrate her ninety-year-old father into her family's Christmas traditions. How will he cope with the clutter and noise of her family, including her toddler grandchildren descending with all their energy on the home he is just beginning to feel comfortable in after years of independent living? Will he feel left out if he stays in another room to avoid the confusion? Will the family understand if he chooses not to partake of their celebration filled with traditions he has never been a part of but now can't avoid? And, in this wintry season, a seemingly minor decision could lead to tension: Should she set the thermostat for the comfort of his aging body or for those active enough not to need the extra heat? For years she has successfully juggled her multiple roles as wife, mother and grandmother; this year, she would integrate another role, never forgotten but now changing: adult daughter.

In our younger days we begged our parents to see us and treat us as adults; now, when they do, we squirm at the demands of the role. We are hesitant about shedding our own dependence to shoulder some of theirs. Their sometimes helplessness saddens us as we make the obvious link between their aging and their mortality.

We must allow them to quit the pedestal where they've been enshrined—not in a fall from grace, but in a graceful, gradual descent. With dignity intact, they ask us to be their partners as they close out their lives. Moving through aging with them may be our last and best gift to them—if we can walk gently, patiently and lovingly—in return for their countless acts of love toward us, their now-grown children.

❧ BEGINNING TODAY... I will try to be patient with the mental and physical pace of my aging parents. If my friends face difficult decisions about their older parents' futures, I will lend a sympathetic ear as they struggle to be loving adult children.

Facing Death

...in every being's ideas of death, and his behavior when it suddenly menaces him, lies the best index to his life and his faith.—Herman Melville, Redburn

N o one can truly grasp the depths of loss, since each death cuts a singular, personal swath in the heart, but those who have experienced death in their own families know something of the pain. They know that they can't really know; they know there's little comfort in "I know how you feel."

A death—of a child, a spouse, an intimate friend, a parent—marks a turning point in our lives, a line of demarcation by which we measure and remember events. No matter how stormy the relationship was in life, no matter how relieved we are that the suffering is over (for the dead one, for ourselves), we could never have imagined before the death what our lives would be like after it. Those who have not endured the waiting, the early morning phone calls, the false alarms, the tentativeness of plans for those still living are among the uninitiated; they stand outside the community of grievers.

Urged on by an unspoken bond, the community helps the healing begin. Word spreads quickly among them, not merely to pass along the information, but to set in motion a support system to help those devastated by death navigate the first few days of mourning. No matter how pressing their own affairs, fellow grievers find the time to write a note of comfort, run errands that can't wait, prepare food for a family that still must eat, pray at the wake or stand silently at the graveside to bid farewell.

And they are there later, at the first social gathering when death should be on no one's mind, to ask "How are you doing?" when others lack the courage to raise the much-needed question. They are there at the first empty holidays, or on the anniversary of the death, allowing us to speak, to cry, to lament promises unkept or words unspoken. They know that our grieving is not likely to stop, though it may change form, forcing us to confront deaths yet to come, including our own.

Death is the ultimate mystery, the true test of inner resiliency and belief. We have read and heard about a life with God where there will be no more tears, where our souls will no longer be restless because they rest in their source. But do we really believe? And can we ever be truly ready?

Watching older relatives and friends age, I can sense which ones have faced their own mortality. Embracing death with faith puts all other hassles and worries in perspective. I know those who have moved toward that embrace, because they live with a peace that only those who have faced the possibility of their own death can radiate.

Not that they shun life. On the contrary, they savor its little moments and graces because they have grasped the fleetingness of life in this world.

All believers struggle with the demon of death. That became clear during the dying days of Joseph Cardinal Bernardin, who moved openly toward his death, sharing his struggle with the world. Thousands who barely knew him in life came to know and love him in his dying. Commentators in the national media and preachers in their pulpits praised him as a model for all grappling with this universal mystery. And rightly so. But those who knew him intimately said his death was only the capstone of a faith-filled life. Even before his cancer, he had come to grips with essentials in life, so that his death became one more step on the journey.

Like so many others not in the public eye, ordinary people coping with daily moments of life and death, the cardinal had grasped life's continuity. For those who truly believe in a loving God calling us home, the thought of death doesn't stifle life. Their faith is strong enough to see beyond the suffering and fear of this life's end. Their graceful living of life's final days, their concern about our willingness to accept their death, is a gift to us who are still struggling to believe. Their peace is an affirming "amen" to our proclaimed, but sometimes faltering, belief in a "world without end."

❧ BEGINNING TODAY... I will make every effort to support those I know who have lost a relative or friend to death: by visiting the funeral home to share hugs and tears, by joining the grievers for the funeral services or by sending a note of consolation. And weeks and months after the funeral, I will continue to be with them as they integrate the pain of their loss into their lives.

Slowing Down

But I have calmed and quieted my soul.—Psalm 131:2

"I really don't want to go on medication. Please, please, give me a chance to get my blood pressure down," I was pleading with my family doctor during an early morning appointment that I had scurried through the first tasks of my day to keep.

"Stop whining, take a deep breath and calm down so I can get an accurate reading," he laughed, reflecting to me in his response how out-of-control I must sound.

Whether the reading was accurate or not wasn't clear, given my distress during the office visit. My doctor, knowing the history of hypertension in my family, predicted that I'd end up on medication but was willing to give me a chance to prove it wasn't necessary. I could purchase a blood pressure cuff and monitor my levels at home for a few months before we decided.

When the first few readings weren't much better than the ones taken at the doctor's office, I consulted my parents, experts at the process. I was doing it all wrong. First, the ribbing on my shirts could be constricting my arm and giving a false reading. Next, I was too active right before taking the reading.

"I always sit down with a book or music for about ten minutes before I take my blood pressure. Try that," my father suggested.

Oh, sure! Where was I to find ten minutes of inactivity once a day? He was retired, I was an active working woman who barely had time to go to the bathroom each day, much less sit uninterrupted for ten minutes.

But I began to find the time. And my children, unused to my sitting still, began to recognize and respect my ritual. Monitor plopped squarely on the kitchen table in front of me, I'd choose a good book, prop my feet up, and relax...for ten minutes. I had the perfect excuse: "I have to relax to take my blood pressure." Almost as good as my no longer valid reason for staying put: "I can't come right now, I'm nursing the baby."

When had my life gotten so complicated that I needed to plan time to relax, and then make excuses for it? What was filling up my days? Was all this rushing around really essential? Certainly some activities couldn't be eliminated, like trips to the pharmacy to refill prescriptions or to the doctor for myself or others, events at the parish, carpools for scouts or sports and the daily demands of my career.

But too many times I seem to be running in place, wearing myself out with little to show in the end. The elevated blood pressure should have been a clue that my body was having a hard time keeping up with the demands I was placing on it. It was the wake-up call I've needed.

I've begun to slow down, I really have. The withdrawal won't happen overnight. A friend—a teacher but not a parent, so I valued her objective stance—once asked me a pivotal question: "Why do you have to go to every game your kids play? Can't they enjoy sports without you? Did your parents attend every event you participated in?"

Her questions were challenging and freeing. What would happen if I didn't take in every practice? If other parents drove them to games across town? And from these, other questions, probably more important in building habits and setting the tone for the rest of my life: What would happen if I began taking time for myself? Why wait for retirement to read a book for pleasure, to take brisk walks with my dog, to go shopping just for the joy of it?

Without time to shake the dust from my soul, without inner quiet, how can I bring peace to those I love? I know this hectic pace is nothing I have a corner on and, although some of the present clutter in my life is related to being a mother, overcrowding is not a "mother" state; it afflicts most women I know today who haven't given themselves permission to slow down and savor life.

A recent note from a friend, assuring me of prayers during a brief convalescence, reminded me of this frazzle-bond I share with other women. She observed that this "forced 'slow down' time to heal during December was also a 'gift'—you were given the rare opportunity to take in the true beauty and loving spirit of the season rather than be rush, rush, frantic, crazed people." It was a gift, and it was one of my most meaningful Christmases of recent memory, but it's a gift more women need to give themselves rather than fall into because of circumstances in their lives.

What we envy should be a clue to how our lives should change. What I need are more walks in the woods or the park so that I really notice the changing seasons, more "wasted" time with people I love, the luxury of savoring a favorite passage from Scripture, leisurely breakfasts, a thick Sunday paper and another cup of coffee.

I can dream of a less stressful life—or I can begin to ease into it. Of course, I'm not retired like my father who reminded me to sit still and listen to music, but this tightrope act called my life doesn't have to be as precarious as I'm making it. My life can be more relaxing, more useless, if I make choices to move it in that direction.

All it takes is that first non-step.

❧ BEGINNING TODAY... I will take time to waste time. I will do something frivolous, something totally useless to slow myself down. I will breathe deeply and savor this time away from chores and commitments.

Renewed in Nature

The heavens are telling the glory of God; and the firmament proclaims his handiwork.—Psalm 19:1

T hat the snow came was no surprise, given the increasingly urgent weather warnings flickering across the television screen all day. But how much and how quickly it fell caught me off guard. Through yard lights and porch lights I watched it swirl as I awakened during the night to check on the storm's progress. By the light of morning, I was overwhelmed at the transformation of a winter-dingy neighborhood to snow-shrouded landscape.

Layers of snow hid cars, curbs and bushes. The once familiar was now eerily unfamiliar. Looking out the window I saw the earth in its newness, the freshness of nature still unblemished. Later as I shoveled, new snow fell, thwarting my efforts but restoring the pristine whiteness I had awakened to.

In days to come, as I grumbled about the long lines at the grocery stores, plans sabotaged by event cancellations, muscles aching from grueling hours of shoveling, I tried to recapture the wonder of that snowy morning. The quiet and the beauty had touched me. But more than that: The massiveness, the power of the snowfall had connected me with the sacred.

I have felt the same stirrings of reverence in settings quite different from that wintry one. One summer, under the shelter of a porch overlooking Lake Michigan, bundled in jacket and blankets, I watched with awe as storm clouds rolled toward me and ten-foot waves crashed against beaches where hours earlier I had dug sand castles and complained of the heat of the sun.

In another spot and another time, waking before dawn and scurrying outside just in time, I caught the first rays of the sunrise over the ocean. The horizon was breathtaking in its expansiveness, the night's darkness giving way to the pastel rays of the new day. No crashing breakers this time, but power in the gentleness of waves lapping against a beach speckled with sea glass and shells. Near the shore I was startled by movement not far away: four dolphins leaping through the waters, their arched flight a dance of praise celebrating the glory of the morning.

Naming the emotion of these nature events is not easy. One woman, a poet from the past, had special gifts of sight and insight when it came to nature. Though many of her readers think of Emily Dickinson's life as narrowly inscribed by her house in New England, she understood nature beyond those walls in its profoundness. Not a woman willing to be bound by religion, she had little use for the rituals and rules of the faith of her fathers, but she had a keen grasp of the sacred. I revere her as a woman deeply spiritual in her probing the wonders of creation. Through her poems that read like miniature prayers celebrating the mystery of the world around her, this woman wordsmith helps me articulate the renewing force that nature has been in my life.

On winter, late-afternoon walks, I hear her words: "There's a certain Slant of light, /Winter Afternoons...When it comes, the Landscape listens—/Shadows—hold their breath" and I feel at once the beauty and oppression of the winter-lighted landscape; the experience and her words that capture it so perfectly draw me out of my reverie and my problems as I pause really to see what I am seeing, the path I take often and too often take for granted.

On an early morning run to the edge of my driveway to retrieve the daily paper, I unbend to catch a glimpse of a faint streak in the eastern sky. I am breathless, and wordless, but Emily's words capture the gift of that morning vision: "I'll tell you how the sun rose,—/A ribbon at a time."

She was right when she wrote "Nature is Harmony—/Nature is what we know—/Yet have no art to say—/So impotent Our Wisdom is/ To her Simplicity." Perhaps I should feel humbled in the face of the simple beauty that surrounds me and the paucity of my language to describe it. But instead of feeling insignificant when confronted with such harmony, my often-complex life becomes simpler and fuller, easier to bear, in its renewed energy and significance. With each immersion in nature, I touch a godhead that includes rather than excludes, that enriches me as I'm enveloped in its power. Although I can't quite agree with Emily that "Nature is Heaven," I sense in these moments that nature gives us a glimpse of the harmony of eternity. These brushes with the divine rekindle my sense of the magnitude and magnanimousness of my God.

❧ BEGINNING TODAY... I will renew myself in nature, no matter what the weather or season. I will look closely at the sunrise or flowers or insects to rediscover the divine through creation. I will drink deeply of the textures, smells and sounds of the world around me: the bite of a winter wind, the aroma of a lilac bush, the bark of tree. For all these and for my renewal through them, I will praise God.

Letters

I am lonely and sad, weary of staying here. Would love to sleep in Jesus. You know not what it is to be afflicted as I am. Write me a good letter. You can if the Lord will. Please do write soon to your dear Thera and the Lord bless you.—1863 letter from Thera Weaver to Melissa Case

T here wasn't much extraordinary about these two women, residents of New England in the mid-nineteenth century. Neither is famous enough to have been preserved in history books: One lived in Massachusetts and one in Connecticut. They had met several summers at camp meetings, where they praised God together and formed a deep friendship. What was extraordinary was the barriers they faced in keeping those summer friendships alive. Barriers like a highway system that was less a system than a random series of plank roads that often began in one state then abruptly ended at the state line, neighboring officials having failed to communicate plans for the route of the intended link. Or a wartime economy that forced young women to work to help support large families or pay board at their rooming houses, so they could ill afford to take time off from work or had little money for train fare (if, indeed, the trains connected the cities where they lived).

But what a gift they had in the postal system, primitive by our standards today—what a bargain and link to their friendship. Those summer camp meeting friendships survived many years through Melissa's and Thera's letters.

Although I have not read Melissa's letters to Thera, I know how much they meant to Thera, who was sick much of her adult life, plagued by typhoid fever and other diseases doctors had not yet learned to control. In her suffering, she found comfort in her friend's letters.

Today, many of us have forgotten the solace and richness of the written word shared between friends. Long newsy letters seem somehow obsolete in this age of instant communication. Not only are there jets and freeways to keep us connected, but more instantly we can connect through fax machines, beepers and cellular phones. All of them help nurture our friendships.

Perhaps I'm biased, writer that I am, but I still perceive a permanence to the written word that can't be duplicated by more modern forms of communication. Among my most treasured possessions are letters written by friends during memorable times of my life: hospitalization of my children, the death of my pet, my mother's illness, promotions at work or significant birthdays.

When it comes to most other clutter around my home, I'm a pitcher not a saver. As soon as the newspaper is read, it's in the recycling bin; clothes, too tight or unworn for a year or two, find a home in someone else's closet. So I'm somewhat deviant in holding onto letters from special people. Even though I've read their messages dozens of times, they're treasures I just can't part with.

Letter-writing, personal not business, seems a distinctively feminine mode of communication. Of course, men have always written letters. We have volumes of correspondence from American statesmen. A few of these letters, such as John Adams's to his wife Abigail, strike me as warm and personal, but most I've read are records of national business or policy. It's not difficult for me to imagine these men writing all their letters with an eye toward future generations' judgments on them. In contrast, most women from years past, aware that their lives were considered relatively insignificant in shaping the politics of the world, wrote about details of their lives, sharing words, no matter how ill-formed, from their hearts.

Today, we don't write as many letters, preferring the immediacy of technology. But we still send written communication. Perhaps it's not terribly original or polished, maybe it's just a greeting card with a note. From my random survey of browsers in the aisles of card stores, one of my favorite getaway spots, my guess is that the greeting card industry would close its doors without women. Even though someone else has written the verse inside the cards, if you choose carefully, you can find a message that matches your mood.

Then there's a newer form of written communication: electronic mail. Some call it impersonal. A friend jokes about how we send e-mail to our colleagues down the hall, when we know they're at their desks. But for me, e-mail has been a link to friends present and past. Former students, now professionals with access to this form of letter-writing, communicate with me over cyberspace from across the country. Friends at work use e-mail to share whimsical stories and profound insights which would have evaporated before they remembered to tell me in the hallways. One longtime friend, who lives in the same city but by a different clock than I, shares her thoughts electronically at her peak hours and I retrieve them at mine. No matter what form my friends' messages take, if they're written, I cherish them.

Just recently I ran into a friend who, having known my

mother in years past, sent her a get-well card with a brief note promising prayers for healing. What a surprise when she received a letter in return. "I've read it over and over," she shared warmly. "Imagine, I'd written to cheer her up and she sends me a letter that has cheered me."

The earliest Christians wrote letters to keep alive the spirit of Jesus, to work out difficulties among themselves and build up their fledgling community. Today, we have other media to help us achieve those goals, but there's still a need in our modern community for the written word. Letters, in an enduring way, provide warmth and cheer we can cherish and revisit whenever our drooping spirits need a lift. Letters, in a special way, help keep the members of the Body whole.

❧ BEGINNING TODAY... I'll invest in greeting cards or a box of notepaper and stamps and keep them near my address book. During a lull at work or home I'll drop a friend or relative a short note or take time later in the day to write a newsy letter. If I'm more comfortable with electronic mail, I'll use that technology to speed a personal greeting to someone who's in need of cheer.

'Girl Talk'

*MRS. HALE: It's a log cabin pattern. Pretty, isn't it? I
wonder if she was goin' to quilt it or just knot it?
[Footsteps have been heard coming down the stairs. The
SHERIFF enters followed by HALE and the COUNTY
ATTORNEY.] SHERIFF: They wonder if she was going
to quilt it or just knot it!
[The men laugh, the women look abashed.]—Susan
Glaspell,* Trifles

We had come together early one morning, three
women who knew each other somewhat as
friends, but more as professional colleagues, to
flesh out a proposal we had been kicking around in our
conversations about an issue we believed in deeply. Since
we realized our stand might meet resistance, we wanted to
talk it through and commit it to paper for others to consider.
Coffee mugs in hand, we sat down to shape our argument,
but before we could pursue the topic that had brought us
together, our conversation leapt off-track. We slipped into
talk about leg hair.

Yes, leg hair. Afterwards, I tried to recreate the
discussion to discover just how we had moved to this topic
(which we eventually dropped to continue the real point of
the meeting). I never could. In the years since, I have
savored that moment, not because of any new information I
had gained on leg hair, but because of the utter absurdity
yet profound symbolism of that conversation. Here we
were, three professional women, myself the junior in the
group that ranked among the more respected in our

institution, gathered for intensely serious business, but talking candidly, without embarrassment, about something so seemingly trivial. From one woman I learned that she wore pants as far into the year as she could; the other shared that after menopause she no longer had to shave her legs. These tidbits I would mull over and tuck away for future personal reference.

But it was the tone rather than the topic that intrigued and charmed me. How was it that the three of us, so different in background and personality, could slip easily into a discussion seemingly insignificant, yet ultimately intimate? Do men ever talk like this at work, I began to wonder. Not, of course, about leg hair specifically, but about personal issues of the body. Or was it because we are women that we felt comfortable with "girl talk," a phrase meant to be demeaning in its connotations, but implying a powerful bond that men might not be able to imagine.

In her 1920 play *Trifles*, Susan Glaspell weaves the plot of a murder mystery around the power of women's conversation, frivolous to the male authority figures (the sheriff and the county attorney) who overhear it, but in reality the key to unraveling the murder. Though the sheriff can find no clues to support a case against the dead man's wife, in the homely details of the wife-suspect's kitchen, the women find the key to the case: in spoiled preserves, dirty kitchen towels, a dead canary and an unfinished quilt. The men, unable to grasp the significance of these details, leave the scene of the crime without the evidence they're seeking, even though they're convinced the wife is the murderer.

"Girl talk," "trifles," "gossip," "kitchen talk." Through the years, women's words have been relegated to the devalued pole of talk, in opposition to "serious talk" or "weighty conversation." Rather than two poles, I prefer to think of conversation as situated on a continuum. It's not either-or, trivial vs. meaningful. One point of talk should flow smoothly into the next level of meaning. It's not leg hair vs. issues of substance, but a fluid shifting back and forth between one and the other. In cutting through artificial categories of talk, women are able to get at the heart of issues quickly. Once the facades have been stripped away, once women have acknowledged their commonality on one level, they can transfer that to another.

That early morning leg-hair coffee klatch (as it might have been perceived if someone had been eavesdropping) moved naturally into a drafting of a letter, at once creative and effective. We wrote the proposal, then eventually worked through the roadblocks we knew it would meet. We achieved our original goal.

Perhaps the same goal would have been accomplished if we had moved directly into the work at hand without our opening discussion. But I prefer to think not. We had begun by breaking down barriers. Knowing that no topic would be taboo with our group, we had nothing to lose in speaking openly about our mission, laying out our own fears about its acceptability and anticipating the objections of others.

Over the years, perhaps on the tongues of males like Glaspell's mocking investigators, powerful words about women have been diminished. Today's "gossip" is a devalued version of its linguistic ancestor, the Middle English *godsib*, which meant close friend, godparent or godchild. I like the archaic version better. From my perspective no conversation is trivial if it forges links between minds and souls, whether it's about prize-winning scientific theories, babies' sleeping habits or leg hair. It's in the connecting that we maintain our friendships; it's in the sharing that we parent one another on our mutual journey toward God.

&❧ BEGINNING TODAY... I will listen to and share conversation with others on any topic and not dismiss it as insignificant. I will be especially attentive to women who seem disconnected from me and other women, in hopes of building some bridges between our lives.

Links to Our Past

If I die, don't take me to the cemetery....
Sprout seeds for me. I want them growing
in the yellow chalk of my bones.
I'll climb the roots like a grey staircase, and watch you
from the purple lilies.—Juana de Ibarbourou, "Life-Hook"

T hey are still with us, even though they have been counted among the dead for decades or for centuries. They live among us in their own words and others' words about them. These women from the past survive today among women who turn to them for inspiration, claiming a legacy they had ignored for too long. Women today are eager to rediscover their forebears through letters, pictures, art—anything to link us to those who helped pave our way. As we seek to understand ourselves as women, we reach back, reclaiming our ancestors' stories.

The women we champion as our personal heroes will be different for each of us, but in the sharing we will piece together a kind of friendship quilt to remind us of our heritage. To this sisterly quilting bee, I bring snippets from the fabrics of the lives of a trinity of women I admire: Each has touched God in her own way, and each has helped me understand how my life is interwoven with the lives of those around me.

Julian of Norwich. Years before I discovered her, others had already been touched by this woman born in the fourteenth century. She's not my usual kind of hero, a mystic who prayed that she would experience sickness so that she could know the passion of Christ, and God answered her prayer. Her revelations came on what some thought would be her deathbed...but she lived many more years, sharing with others what she had learned about God.

Of the insights she communicated in *Revelations of Divine Love*, two speak especially to me. The first reminds me simply of the nature of God's love. In this revelation, Julian had an image of something tiny, the size of a hazelnut, in the palm of her hand. When she asked what it was, the answer came back: "It is everything that is made." Realizing that something so small might easily disintegrate, Julian came to understand that everything ever created continues to exist only because of God's love.

Another one of her visions reveals a God that I can more easily relate to than the God perpetuated by Church fathers. In her vision of the Trinity, Julian dismisses the male-only version of God. The God of her visions possesses three attributes: Fatherhood, Motherhood and Lordship. "[T]he deep wisdom of the Trinity is our Mother," she believed, and "just as truly as God is our Father, so too God is our Mother." This image, startling in its modernity, helps me relate to a richly genderless God.

Elizabeth Ann Seton. She knew how to love. Although I rejoiced the day she was canonized as the first native-born American saint, I hoped this official recognition of her virtue would not serve us all badly by diminishing her humanity. I had grown up hearing of her life and virtues, singing of this early-nineteenth-century "valiant woman" in a grade school musical celebrating her life. Only as I matured, experiencing my own loves, did I really begin to connect with her spirituality, based so firmly in the basics of the gospel.

I feel the love of Christ in Elizabeth's love for children, especially poor children, in her reputation as pioneer of the American parochial school system. I know of her love for her sisters in Christ, through her status as "Mother" Seton, founder of an order of religious nuns. But I identify most with her in her other loves—as a small child, grieving for her dead mother; as daughter devoted to her father, physician to sick immigrants; as wife to William, whom she watched waste away and die in a foreign land where they had journeyed to find health; as mother to five children, several of whom were to become her "sisters" in their Emmitsburg, Maryland, convent, several of whom she held in her arms as they died; as dear friend, able to nurture and sustain love even over distances and years. As Saint Elizabeth Ann Seton, I admire her; as Elizabeth Ann Bayley Seton, woman, I connect with her in the amazing richness of her life.

Harriet Ann Jacobs. "I was born a slave." Those words begin a remarkable autobiography by a nineteenth-century woman who may have been a slave in the eyes of the law but who had an inner freedom and dignity that no one could rob her of. Her faith in God and the friendship of women in her life helped her through tests to her humanity and her womanhood. She was cursed with beauty—cursed, because it was bad enough being a slave, but being a slave woman brought an additional burden: the lust of the white slave owner. Day after day, she was subjected to the sexual advances of her master. To foil him in his quest for her body, she used her brain: She deliberately became pregnant by another white man and bore his children. Still a slave, rather than giving in to the slave owner's continued advances, she traded her "easy" life in his home in the city for life on a plantation. When the time was right, she planned her escape, much to the chagrin of her owners.

She could have done like other slaves and fled to safety in the north, but she wouldn't leave without her children. So, aided by her grandmother who had raised her, she hid in a cramped garret above her grandmother's house; for seven years, unbeknownst to her children, supported by her grandmother and other friends, she glimpsed their daily lives through a peephole, watching them grow, hearing them pine for their lost mother, learning of their days in jail and their sale to other owners. Years later, in the north, still not free because of the Fugitive Slave Act that permitted bounty hunters to return runaway slaves, she was eventually reunited with her family. She could have been bitter— especially at the God in whose name slavery was so often justified, but she saw through the trappings of religion to the truth of the Bible, which was her source of consolation as she waited for freedom that came only later in her life.

Mystic, nun, slave—the stark labels hardly do justice to the impact these women have had on my personal and spiritual growth. It is in the telling and retelling of their stories and the stories of so many like them, that we profit from the past. In stitching their stories together, the whole becomes so much bigger than the pieces; we are enriched by the work called "woman" that we continue to create.

2e BEGINNING TODAY... I will learn more about some woman from history who has always been merely a name for me. I will immerse myself in her story and take from it something to help me in my own quest to be a whole and holy woman.

Role Models

*She girds herself with strength, and makes her arms
   strong.*
*She opens her hand to the poor and reaches out her hands
   to the needy.*
*Strength and dignity are her clothing, and she laughs at
   the time to come.*
...let her works praise her at the city gates.—Psalm 31

Flipping through a news magazine, I was not the least
bit surprised to read that the "10 Most Powerful"
people in America were men. Power doesn't seem to
be what most women are pursuing these days, at least not
the women in my life. Another category in the same article,
the "25 Most Influential," yielded different results: Eight
women had made the list, among them a supreme court
justice, a talk show host, a psychologist and a rock singer.
Influential in the nation, possibly, but if they had touched
my life, it had been only remotely.

I have my own list of the influential, those women who
have helped shape my values, offered direction when I was
faltering, set examples through their courage. All have
helped me keep my life on course, much more so than any
talk show host or rock singer. Here are a few.

"Earth Saver." She's a family friend, my former college
teacher, who has redirected her energies to educating
beyond the classroom walls. Her mission: to convince others
to save the earth which the Creator has entrusted to us, a
mission she feels we're botching pretty badly. But she hasn't
despaired. Despite the gloomy predictions about ozone

layers, rain forest destruction, environmental pollution, she continues to celebrate life and to believe in the redemptive possibilities of a community effort. Unimpressed with her credentials, she rolls up her sleeves and shows others how to insulate their homes, recycle materials, use their energy to save the earth's. Her gift of making scientific data understandable to the scientifically-illiterate, her passion for her cause and her simple belief that Providence guides her life inspire me to reassess whether I am "living simply so others may simply live."

"Justice Seeker." Another family connection, a friend of my sister's from childhood, whom I'd known only briefly in our growing-up years. By some fluke, we'd both gravitated to the same city, the same neighborhood, the same parish, where she has immersed herself in issues of peace and justice. She's no fanatic, though some might label her that in her relentless and single-minded devotion to promoting the gospel. Armed with information and principles she's gleaned from Scripture and the documents of the Catholic Church, coupling action with prayer, she launches her nonviolent battle against whatever oppresses, whether it's domestic abuse or guns. Her vision is truly a "seamless garment" approach to supporting life in all its forms, from before birth to death. She knows she's a nuisance to some, the nagging prophet among those who want to hide from tough issues. So when she submitted an article to the parish newsletter detailing her approach to life issues, she could jokingly headline it "Oh, no, not her again!" She can laugh at herself and others' perception of her while she continues to take her causes seriously.

"Word Wizard." She could have been a powerful media woman, but she chose to return to the less auspicious role of writer. An influential newspaper editor for several years, she gave up the title and management duties to do what she did best: Use words to tell others' stories. Trained not only as a writer but also as a counselor, she's able to speak for those who cannot speak. When she interviews the weak or the powerful, she identifies so strongly with their joys and their pain that the story is always more than just another assignment. After a trip to an impoverished country to write about poor women eking out a living, she returned to the states with much more than a story to write: She had a trunkload of their crafts to sell. She was shameless in hosting an open house to sell their handmade goods: Christmas stockings, eyeglass cases, wall hangings. Those who bought the gifts came away with something besides colorful treasures; they were richer for having heard the story of other women's struggles and triumphs. In print or in person, my writer friend communicates not only through finely honed phrases but through her value-laden life.

"Value Anchor." Thirty years ago, I would never have dreamed that she'd still be a part of my life, still influencing my values. And I would never have hoped that she'd be my friend. We started off in a relationship heavy with the trappings of authority—she the director of novices of a women's religious community and I an impressionable young novice. But her authority was never oppressive, I came to understand only later, when I heard horror stories from other novices, in the same community and others, about the tactics of novice directors who demanded "blind obedience" of the young. Although we abided by congregational rules demanded of new members, she brought a humanness to our search for sanctity. Thirty years ago she modeled and taught what is accepted wisdom today: that holiness means wholeness. Today, when I sit in meetings with her, or listen to her reflect on Scripture at a friend's fiftieth anniversary as a nun, or meet in the hall for a quick greeting, I realize what a centering influence she has been over the decades I've known her. Her wisdom, her spiritual vision, her humanity reinforce my own quest to lead a whole and happy life in my search for God.

There have been others, of course, who have bolstered me along the way. Each woman should have her own list, and be gracious enough to be on others' lists, no matter how uncomfortable that role may be. In many ways, my influential women are nothing extraordinary. They have their own struggles unknown to those who admire them. Like others, they probably worry about overdue bills or the health of their families or troubled personal relations. They've known frustration and anger and sadness, just like many women in the world. They didn't ask to be role models, and they'd be embarrassed to be singled out. Their self-effacement is what makes them attractive to me and other women. I can emulate them, but I dare not canonize them. At least not yet.

ಶ BEGINNING TODAY... I will reflect on women who have been models in my life. Without embarrassing them, I will let them know how their values and courage have been an inspiration to me as I strive for holiness.